D1443689

Clans & Tartans

Clans & Tartans

James Mackay

GRAMERCY BOOKS
NEW YORK

ACKNOWLEDGMENTS

The publisher wishes to thank following for kindly supplying the photography for this book:

© David Lyons/Event Horizons for pages 2, 6-7, 8-9, 10-11, 13, 14, 15, 16-17, 18, 19 (both), 20, 21, 22-23 (all), 24, 25, 26, 27, 28 (all), 29, 30, 31, 32, 34, 37 (bottom), 40-41, 42 (bottom), 43 (bottom), 45 (bottom), 48 (top), 51, 52 (bottom), 54 (bottom), 61, 64 (top), 70 (bottom), 72-73, 74, 77, 80-81, 86-87, 88-89, 92-93, 96-97, 102-103, 112-113, 115, 116-117, 121, 123, 125 and 127.

All the tartans in this book were provided by the Scottish Tartans Society, Port-na-Craig Road, Pitlochry, Perthshire PH16 5ND.

For front and back jacket acknowledgments see flaps.

© 2000 by PRC Publishing Ltd.

All rights reserved under International and Pan-American Copyright Conventions.

No part of this book may be reproduced or transmitted in any form or by any means electronic or mechanical including photocopying, recording, or by any information storage and retrieval system, without permission in writing from the publisher.

This 2000 edition is published by Gramercy Books™,
an imprint of Random House Value Publishing, Inc.,
280 Park Avenue, New York, NY 10017,
by arrangement with PRC Publishing Ltd,
Kiln House, 210 New Kings Road, London, SW6 4NZ.

Gramercy Books™ and design are trademarks of
Random House Value Publishing, Inc.

Printed and bound in China

Random House
New York • Toronto • London • Sydney • Auckland
http://www.randomhouse.com/

A catalogue record for this book is available from the Library of Congress.

ISBN 0-517-16240-7

8 7 6 5 4 3 2 1

CONTENTS

INTRODUCTION

The Welsh word *plant* meaning seed (from the Latin *planta*) became transformed in *Goidelic* (Q-Celtic) to *cland*. From *cland* comes the Gaelic word *clann*, originally meaning seed and from this acquiring its modern meaning of children. The notion of people belonging to a family, tribe, or even an entire race as the children of a common ancestor is to be found all over the world (as in, for instance, the Jews regarding themselves as the children of Israel). Modern anthropologists have hijacked the word "clan"; the *Encyclopaedia Britannica*, for example, defines it as "a social group of fundamental importance in the social structure of many primitive societies," and in the text that follows the only reference to the word in its original meaning is a side-swipe at "that rather vague entity, the Scottish clan" which, for reasons unexplained, does not apparently fit into the modern sociological concept.

Well, that's as may be, but we are here concerned with the clan in its original sense of a kindred group. Celtic society was organized on family lines which were reflected in laws, customs, and systems of land-holding. Traces of these may be found in many countries, wherever Celtic tribes left their mark in their westward migration across central Europe in pre-Christian times. Vestiges of this ancient system survived in the remotest parts of the continent, on the western fringes of the British Isles, in Wales, Ireland, and the Highlands of Scotland.

In Ireland the head of a family would adopt the word *Ua* (grandson) followed by the name of an ancestor, as in *Ua Suilleabhain* which became Anglicized as O'Sullivan. The chief would simply be known by that name, while his followers would take it as a surname after their chosen forenames. In Scotland, Wales, and also in Ireland, surnames were originally formed simply

Right: Detail of a Pictish stone in Aberlemno graveyard, Tayside.

by adding details of a person's father, and sometimes grandfather as well. Thus James the son of John, son of Donald was known in Gaelic as *Seumas mac Iain mhic Domhnuill*. In the case of a woman, Mary the daughter of John, son of Donald would be *Mairi nighean Iain mhic Domhnuill*, though as a rule the word *nighean* (daughter) was shortened in surnames to *nic*.

In the Anglicized forms of Highland surnames Mac is used for both sexes, but if you study the credits at the end of Gaelic programs on television you will see that female surnames often begin with Nic. It should be noted that in Welsh (P-Celtic) the word for son was rendered as *map*, but the initial consonant disappeared, so that surnames developed as *Ap*, as in *Ap Rhys* (son of Rhys), Anglicized as Price or Preece. In Manx (Q-Celtic) Mac likewise became eroded, leaving only the final consonant, rendered as C, K, or Qu, as in *Clucas* (son of Lucas), *Kermode* (son of Dermot or Diarmid) and *Quilliam* (son of William).

The gradual adoption of surnames in Scotland in the thirteenth and fourteenth centuries developed the idea that all persons who bore a particular surname were somehow related through some common ancestor, hence the emphasis on the word *clann* (children). The word *siol* (seed) was also used, either to denote a division in a large clan such as the MacLeods whereby the MacLeods of Lewis (*Siol Thorcuil*) and MacLeods of Harris and Skye (*Siol Thormoid*) traced their descent from Torquil and Tormod, the sons of Leod in the thirteenth century. The term is also used to denote a confederation of clans which trace their descent from a common ancestor, such as *Siol Alpin* which embraces the Grants, Macaulays, Macfies, Macgregors, Mackinnons, Macnabs, and Macquarries.

In its purest form the clan was essentially a family group whose members traced their roots back to a common ancestor and who were therefore linked by

Left: Clach Mhicleoid (Clan Macleod) standing stone near Horgabost, Isle of Harris, looking southwest.

blood ties. It included all illegitimate children—so long as their fathers acknowledged paternity—as well as children adopted or fostered by the family. It might also include the children of women who had married outside the family group and who, therefore, bore a different surname. More commonly, however, the appearance of other surnames within the clan arose as a result of landless men or outlaws attaching themselves to the clan for protection, rendering service in return. From this arose the notion of the sept. This word, derived from the Latin *septum*, a fence or enclosure, alludes to the fact that, originally, a certain piece of clan land was set aside for these landless followers where they could establish a village of their own. Rather confusingly, the Gaelic word for a sept is *fine*, often used indiscriminately to denote a clan, tribe, or kindred. In Ireland *Fine Gael* is the name of one of the major political parties. A number of clans do not have gaelic equivalent names, this is because they have non-Highland origins and are instead of English or Norman stock (like Barclay and Ramsay), or because the clan has never been based in the Highlands.

Although the clan system in Scotland was smashed in the aftermath of the Jacobite Rebellion of 1745–46 the age-old allegiance of the clansman to his chief was gradually replaced by the ties of kindred, in which the possession of a common surname became of paramount importance. Your surname gives you a sense of identity, but in the Scottish system it also provides a feeling of solidarity that nowadays links people from every part of the globe and every walk of life. The ties that bind us may be extremely tenuous, or even quite spurious, but the name is all-important. The spread of Scottish clan names to every part of the world is a reflection of the Scottish diaspora. It has been estimated that there are over 30 million people outside Scotland who are of Scottish descent—six times the number of people actually residing in

Left: Tartan-uniformed pipe band at the Braemar Gathering.

Scotland. Pride in bearing a Scottish surname has not only strengthened the bonds of expatriates, whether in communities which have retained their Scottish character or those living in isolated groups, but has also helped to keep alive a sense of Scottish nationhood over the past three centuries. Now that Scotland has regained a measure of political autonomy, this sense of Scottishness is enjoying a renaissance, at home as well as abroad.

Possession of a Scottish surname entitles you to wear the tartan of your clan. Even if your surname is not that one of the hundred or so great clans, the chances are that you bear the surname of one of the numerous septs. In relatively recent years the notion has arisen that, in default of a clan or sept surname, you can wear the tartan of your mother's clan (or grandmother's for that matter). Purists and sticklers for tradition argue against this widespread practice, pointing out that there are perfectly good alternatives. As a subject of Her Majesty the Queen, for example, you could wear Royal Stewart tartan to show your allegiance. If you balk at that on political or nationalist lines, then you could wear the Caledonia tartan, cunningly devised in the nineteenth century to embrace all people of Scotland, or even the Jacobite tartan, allegedly worn by the clanless followers of Bonnie Prince Charlie. There are even occupational tartans designed to be worn by shepherds or ministers of religion, and if all else fails there is even the Burns check (actually invented by a Frenchman, and designed to be worn by fans of Robert Burns).

Clan names bob up in the unlikeliest of places. There are many Americans of Afro-Caribbean origin who are the bearers of good Scottish surnames, derived from the days of slavery when slaves took the names of their owners or plantation overseers, or as a result of liaisons between masters and their female slaves. The same applies to many people in Bermuda, the Bahamas, and the West Indian islands. I have a distant relative who is descended from our common ancestor, Lachlan Mackintosh, but through the female line ended up with the surname of Brown (as common in Scotland as it is in England). However, by marriage to a West Indian she has acquired a clan name, so the wheel has come full circle. Actually her husband rejoices in the splendid name of Uisdean Clava MacBain: his forename is the Gaelic form of Hugh, while his middle name is a landmark on the battlefield of Culloden near Inverness.

There are also many Scottish names to be found in the telephone books of the Pacific islands and southeast Asia, arising, no doubt, from miscegenation, the mixed marriages of Scottish traders and officials with local girls. A surprisingly large number of "Mac" names will also be found in the directories of every European country. In some cases this arises from movement of population, especially within the European Community, in quite recent years. In many others, however, it goes back to the Thirty Years' War (1618–48) when thousands of Highlanders were recruited by Gustavus Vasa, while many others entered the Garde d'Ecosse and other units in French or Austrian service. After many years of campaigning in every part of Europe Scots often married and settled down. The Mackays of Holland retained their surname (the clan chief eventually became a member of the Dutch peerage) but elsewhere they became transformed into the Von Keys of Sweden and the Makkais of Hungary.

It should also be noted that, while many people in Russia with the surname of Gordon may well be descended from Patrick Gordon of Auchleries (1635–99) who rose to the highest rank in the Russian army under Peter the Great, they are more likely to be Jews deriving their surname from Grodno. Similarly Grant and Morrison are perfectly good Jewish surnames without any connection to the Scottish clans of the same name.

Right: Putting the shot during the Highland Games at the Braemar Gathering.

THE CLAN SYSTEM

Right and Far Right:
Pictish stones in
Aberlemno graveyard,
Tayside.

Few people in Scotland can trace back their roots with any certainty before the beginning of the eighteenth century for the simple reason that parish records seldom exist from an earlier period. Nevertheless, we are all living proof of unknown ancestors who lived thousands of years ago.

Our lineage is every bit as ancient as the Royal Family or the most senior peers of the realm; it's just that our records do not go back as far as theirs. On the other hand, we have clan histories, some of which go back into the very mists of antiquity. Even if we cannot establish our own particular link, we derive some comfort and no little pride from the fact that, on the strength of our surname alone, we can claim kinship

with people who existed a thousand years ago, and in some cases even further back in time.

Clan histories and genealogies (like the gaily colored tartans themselves) are largely a product of the late-eighteenth and early nineteenth centuries. Some far-fetched claims later gave rise to a measure of healthy skepticism regarding these long pedigrees; but a more scholarly approach in recent years, coupled with a systematic study of the vast body of documentary material of all kinds, has served to redress the balance. Two facts are indisputable: Celtic society was organized on tribal lines and the population of Scotland a thousand years ago was very small and often isolated. The popular notion that the Picts somehow died out soon

after they merged with the Scots has now been shown to be quite erroneous, not only in the survival of place-names and artifacts but also in the racial characteristics that are still prevalent in the Highlands. The Picts (from Latin *Picti*, the painted ones) were the oldest established Celtic inhabitants of what is now Scotland, the tribes known to the Romans as the Caledonii and Maeatae. The Scots (*Scotti*) were migrants from northern Ireland who settled in Argyll in the early sixth century and established the kingdom of Dalriada under Fergus Mac Erc and his brothers Lorn and Angus from whom came two of the oldest territorial divisions as well as tribal names.

Descent in the Picts was matrilineal, so when Alpin, King of Scots, married a Pictish princess, their son Kenneth fell heir to both kingdoms and in 843 became King of the Picts and Scots, thus merging the Q-Celtic elements in the lands to the north of the Forth-Clyde isthmus. Southwest Scotland was occupied by the Britons of Strathclyde (P-Celtic, speaking a language akin to Welsh) while the southeast was settled by Anglo-Saxon peoples. Other disparate groups were the Attacotti of Galloway, who retained their individuality till the fifteenth century, and Norse settlements in the far north as well as the islands. Add the Norman merce-naries recruited by King David in the early twelfth cen-tury and the European merchants and traders whose descendants rejoice in such surnames as Fleming (from Flanders), Bremner (from Bremen) and Imrie (from Hungary) and it will be seen that the Scots of the past were a pretty mixed bunch—to say nothing of the pre-sent day Scots whose forebears may have hailed from Ireland in the Hungry Forties, or fled from the pogroms of Tsarist Russia, to say nothing of Italian, Polish, German Jewish, Hungarian, Jamaican, Indian, or Pakistani immigra-tion in the past half century alone.

ALPRAISETOGODAND
THANKIS·TOTHE·MOST
EXCELLENT·MONARCHE
GREAT·BRITANE·OFWH
O SE·PRINCELIE·LIBERA
LITIE·THIS·IS·MV·POR
TIOVNE·DEOLAVS·
☐ ESTO·FIDVS·❀
MDEST·MERCES·
NICOLL·MONCREIF·
⧓ 1 6 1 0·★♥◉

Above: Moncreif house plaque beside Falkland Palace, in Fife, which was built by the Stewarts in the sixteenth century.

Although the clan system of land tenure was established in the Celtic parts of Scotland by the sixth century, if not earlier, the present structure of clans, with identifiable surnames, arose very much later. It was beginning to emerge in the twelfth century and was well established by the 1400s, although in many cases clans trace their origins back to a much earlier (and perhaps mythical) ancestor. Pictland was divided into seven great tribal provinces: Caith (Caithness and Sutherland),

Ce (Mar and Buchan), Ciric (the Mearns), Fibh (Fife), Fidach (Ross and Moray), Fodhla (Atholl), and Fortrenn (west Perthshire). The historian Skene asserted that the basic tribal unit was the *tuath* (tribe), several of which formed a *mortuath* (great tribe). Two or more *mortuaths* formed a *coicidh* (province) which was ruled by a *righ* (from Latin *rex*, a king). These provinces were delineated in such a way that they converged at a central point where the *Ard-Righ* (high king) had his capital at Scone

in Perthshire. The Scots added their tribal districts of Dalriada and together these divisions produced the later clan lands, as well as the counties of more modern times. By the twelfth century there was only one *righ*, but under him the head of the *tuath* was the *toiseach* (a term used in the Republic of Ireland to denote the prime minister), while the head of the *mortuath* was the *mormaer* (great steward).

The clan system was a peculiarly Scottish compromise between the age-old tribal organization and the concepts of feudalism introduced by Margaret, the Anglo-Saxon princess who became the wife of King Malcolm Canmore, and considerably refined and expanded by their sons, with the aid of Norman mercenaries and administrators in the twelfth century. The clans that emerged thereafter were generally subdivisions of the earlier tribes, confined to a particular island, strath, or glen. Over the ensuing centuries, of course, there was a great deal of feuding and fighting, as a result of which some clans became much larger and more powerful than their neighbors. Attempts by successive monarchs to curb the power of the great clans included the occasional punitive expedition, but more often than not chiefs were bought off with grants of land and titles.

By an Act of the Scottish Parliament in 1587 measures were taken for the pacification of the Highlands, Islands, and Borders. Associated with this is the earliest attempt to enumerate the various clans, their chiefs, chieftains, captains, tanists, and other officials, as well as recognition of the fact that clansmen owed their first allegiance to their chiefs. The chief had the power of life and death over his clansmen, but his autocracy was tempered by certain democratic safeguards. He could

Above Left: Detail of statuary above the forecourt of the Palace of Holyroodhouse, in Edinburgh, which was built by the Stewarts in the seventeenth century.

Above: Monument to Bonnie Prince Charlie and the "Forty-Five" at Glenfinnan, where the Young Pretender's standard was raised.

Above: Another view of the Glenfinnan monument.

only make war on another clan with the consent of the whole clan, and he administered the clan lands for the good of all, with an elaborate system of rules along communistic lines.

It was the chief's ability to mobilize his clansmen by sending round the fiery cross that was both his strength and, ultimately, his undoing. Charles II cynically harnessed this powerful warrior class to terrorize the Lowlands into accepting his religious policies. Memories of the depredations of the Highland Host of 1678 remained long and bitter, and help to explain the way in which the country tended to polarize at the time of the Revolution in 1688–90 and again during the Jacobite

rebellions of 1715, 1719, and 1745–46. To be sure, there were clans which supported the House of Orange or the Hanoverian dynasty. The massacre of the Macdonalds of Glencoe by Campbells in 1692 is a prime example of this, just as there were probably as many Highlanders in the army of the Duke of Cumberland at Culloden as in the Jacobite forces ranged against them. But Prince Charles Edward Stuart had derived his strength from the clans and a vengeful government decided that they must be crushed for all time. The power of the chiefs was destroyed by the abolition of heritable jurisdictions in 1747, but those symbols which made the Highlander different from the

Lowlander had also to be eradicated. The wearing of tartan was outlawed in 1746 and Highlanders were compelled to swear an oath that they would give up their Highland garb just as assuredly as they were forced to give up their weapons. Not until 1782 was this legislation revoked, but by that time the Highlander had proved his worth as a soldier in the service of the Crown, the Highland regiments offering the only legitimate outlet for wearing tartan.

The Act of 1747 transformed the clan chief into a landowner. Instead of holding the clan lands in trust, he now became the landlord. In the next generation many chiefs gravitated towards Edinburgh and then London,

content to live off their rents and leave the management of their estates in the hands of tacksmen and factors. In the 1780s began the ruthless process of removing clansmen from the straths and glens to make way for blackface sheep, and when even they proved uneconomic, vast tracts of the Highlands were converted into deer forests, for the sport of wealthy Lowlanders and Sassenachs. The Highland Clearances lasted, off and on, for a hundred years. In the course of the nineteenth century, and especially in the decades after Waterloo (1815), thousands of embittered clansmen and their families emigrated to North America, Australia, and New Zealand, Patagonia and Natal. Not until the 1880s,

Above: Highland cattle.

Right: Memorial cairn on the battlefield of Culloden.

when a royal commission was set up to enquire into conditions in the crofting counties, was this process halted, but by that time it was too late. Today the once silent glens have come to life again, but they are peopled by incomers from the south, from England and even Europe, escaping the rat race, but sometimes by expatriate Scots rediscovering their roots.

CLANS & TARTANS OF SCOTLAND

TARTAN

**Right: Edinburgh
Military Tattoo on the
castle esplanade.**

**Far Right: Portrait of
Norman Macleod,
twenty-second chief of
Clan Macleod, hanging
in Dunvegan Castle,
Skye.**

The "garb of old Gaul" consisted of a piece of woolen cloth, about two meters in width and up to six meters in length, carefully gathered into pleats at the center, one end being wound round the wearer's back, over the shoulder, and secured by a brooch. A stout leather belt secured the garment at the waist and the lower part was pleated and gathered to form the *feileadh beag* or little kilt. From the lower part of this garment developed the *philabeg* or kilt as we know it today, although in its present form it is largely an invention of the eighteenth century.

The origins of the distinctive cloth patterns, which are collectively known as tartan, are shrouded in controversy. To the Gael it was *breacan feile* (speckled cloth) but the word "tartan" appears to come from the French *tirtaine*, implying a European origin. The earliest written

references to tartan occur in the accounts of the treasurer of James III (1471). References to tartan in Gaelic literature date from the early sixteenth century, and descriptions of the different colored cloth appear in Lowland Scots by the 1570s. Martin Martin, writing a century later, commented on the fact that the *sett* (pattern) varied from place to place, so that a person might identify the origins of the wearer from the colors of his cloth. From this it appears that the earliest tartans were territorial rather than clan-based, although in many cases the two would have been synonymous.

The cloth itself was woven and then dyed in a pattern of checks which depended largely on the pigments available locally, the muted greens and russet hues being derived from mosses, lichens, plants, and berries, imported indigo supplying the deep blue shades. The

oldest tartans thus tend to be the darkest—it was the dark blue and green check worn by the government troops policing the Highlands which gave rise to the name of the "Black Watch." From this Government tartan, as it was officially styled, developed many of the other tartans worn by the Highland regiments, varied by the inclusion of contrasting stripes of white, yellow, or red. The Government tartan with a yellow stripe was worn by the Gordon Highlanders, and thus became the Gordon tartan, while the same tartan but with stripes of white and red at right angles was worn by the Seaforth Highlanders and thus became the tartan of the Mackenzies. Other clans whose tartans are similar to the Government tartan include Campbell, Mackay, and Sutherland, while Forbes, Gordon, Lamont, Mackinlay, and Murray tartans have it as a basis on which counterstripes of contrasting colors have been added.

Most of the tartans, as we know them today, date back no further than the 1820s, as a result of two disparate factors. The first was the enterprising firm of Walker of Bannockburn, which held the contract to supply tartan cloth to the Highland regiments at home and abroad, and the second was the visit of King George IV to Scotland in 1822, the first visit north of the Border of the reigning monarch since the time of Charles II. Sir Walter Scott, who stage-managed this event, persuaded the portly monarch to don a kilt, complete with flesh-colored tights. Although the resulting spectacle must have been quite ludicrous, it triggered off the craze for tartan which has endured to this day. It went hand in hand with the romanticism of the Highlands (later fueled by Queen Victoria and Prince Albert) and created a demand for tartans distinctive to every clan, sept, and even the great families of the Borders who had never worn tartan in historical times. Today, each of the hundred-odd clans of Scotland, together with many of their septs, have their own setts; but in many cases variety is imparted by the invention of "ancient" (based on original patterns), "hunting"

Above: Highland dancing at the Braemar Gathering.

Left: Portrait of Dame Flora Macleod, twenty-eighth chief of Clan Macleod, hanging in Dunvegan Castle, Skye.

Top: Highland dancing at the Braemar Gathering.

Above and Right: Throwing the hammer at the Highland Games, Helmsdale.

(muted shades for deer-stalking), and "dress" (suitably flamboyant for evening wear), as well as ordinary tartans for day-wear, so that the number of tartans now runs to many hundreds.

Tartan has developed a heraldry of its own; but even if the colors are not as readily symbolic as the devices on armorial bearings, they are instantly recognizable and identify the wearer's clan. In Atlanta, Georgia, however, I once met a man with an unmistakably German surname who

was sporting a kilt of a particularly gaudy tartan. When I inquired what his connection was with the Buchanan clan, he gave me a quizzical look and replied, "Oh, I simply like the plaid!" Today, tartan has become universal, though sometimes with surprising results. The late Professor Toshio Namba of Tokyo, a Burns scholar of world rank, discovered that his name translated into English as "son of Tosh" and for this reason habitually wore a Mackintosh kilt when attending Burns conferences.

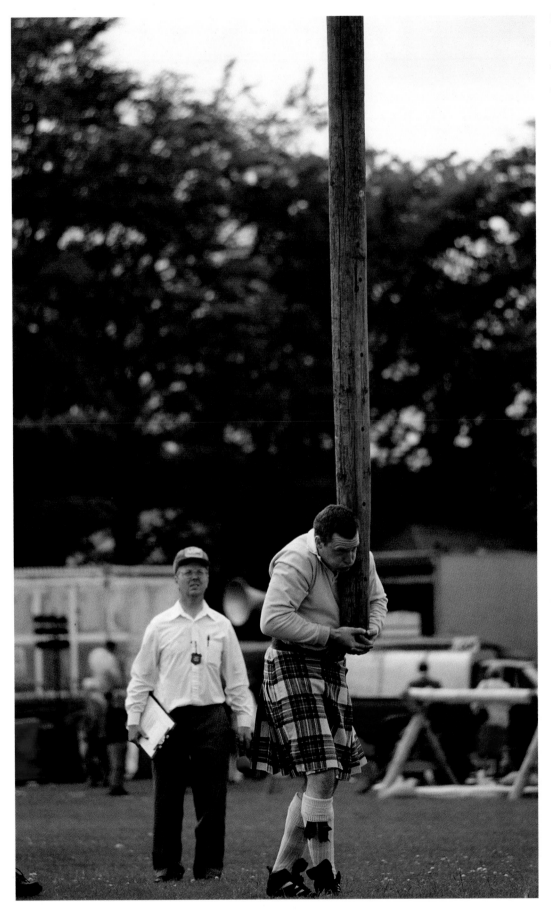

Left: That most Scottish of sports: tossing the caber at the Echt Games, Grampian.

There are hardy souls of my acquaintance whom I have never seen in trousers. In all weathers they wear the kilt and some, for all I know, may do so without underwear in the traditional manner. When I served in the old Highland Light Infantry the wearing of underpants was strictly forbidden, and one of the points of inspection on parade was to lift soldiers' kilts to ensure that they were not breaking Queen's Regulations which stated that undergarments would only be permitted when dancing—and then only with persons of the opposite sex.

For most people, however, the kilt is reserved for special occasions such as Robbie Burns's Birthday (January 25), St. Andrew's Day (November 30), clan gatherings, and Highland games. These four events are now celebrated worldwide and, indeed, some of the largest parades of tartan are to be seen at such spectacular gatherings as the Grandfather Mountain Highland Games in Georgia and the Glengarry Highland Games in Ontario, although there is nothing to beat the Braemar Gathering (attended by the Royal Family from nearby Balmoral) or the Cowal Games for the authentic flavor of piping contests, caber-tossing, hammer-throwing, Highland dancing, and, of course, people-watching.

As for clan gatherings, the descendants of those chiefs who once so callously evicted their tenantry are now honored and revered, not so much for what they are as what they represent; and they, in turn, have become custodians of the clan heritage. Their castles (where they have survived) have become focal points for great reunions or demonstrations of clan solidarity, drawing Scots and hyphenated Scots from all over the world and giving them a sense of oneness and belonging that transcends all barriers of class, creed, and national affiliation.

Above and Left: Pipes and tartan—still symbols of a proud nation.

THE CLANS OF SCOTLAND

There is no hard and fast rule on the spelling of Mac surnames, nor is there any truth whatsoever in the old fallacy that names spelled Mc are Irish and those spelled Mac are Scottish. Both forms are, and have been, used indiscriminately (along with M' which I detest). Tracing my family tree I have found my surname spelled MacKay, McKay, M'Kay, Macky, MacCay, MacY, as well as Mackay. The late Sir Iain Moncreiffe of that Ilk quite properly pointed out that the name should never be spelled MacKay, which implied "son of Kay," when, in fact, the name meant "son of Ay" (*Aodh* in Gaelic). I should, perhaps, point out that MacCoy and McCoy are other variants, as are McKie, Mackie, and McGee. All are perfectly acceptable renderings of the Gaelic *Mac Aoidh*. Similarly, MacIntosh has acquired an intrusive "k," while, conversely, some names may be found spelled MakGill or MakDougal. Gaelic names are translated in the text where possible—i.e. if there is a translation and not just son of . . .

Above: Castle Stalker on Loch Linnhe.

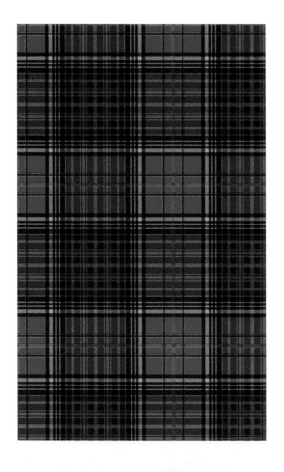

ANDERSON

Badge: An oak tree, with the motto "Stand Sure."
Gaelic: *Mac Ghille Aindreas* (son of the servant or follower of St. Andrew).

This is the usual form of a name found all over Scotland, although its Highland counterpart is Macandrew, a branch of the once-powerful Clan Chattan in Inverness-shire as far back as 1400. Famous clansmen include Dr. John Anderson, founder of the medical college which is now Strathclyde University, and Arthur Anderson, the founder of the P&O shipping line.

ARMSTRONG

Badge: An arm raised in salute, with the Latin motto *Invictus maneo* (I remain unconquered).
Gaelic: *Mac Ghille Laidir* (son of the strong servant).

One of the most powerful of the Border clans, the Armstrongs trace their origin to Fairbairn, a strong man who had the honor of carrying the king's armor and who, according to tradition, was rewarded for his services with lands in Liddesdale. The ballad of Johnny Armstrong recalls the hanging of a famous Border reiver and thirty of his henchmen at Carlingrigg in the reign of James V, though the most famous member of the clan in more recent times is Neil Armstrong, the first man on the Moon.

Right: Smailholm Tower, Borders, is associated with the Armstrong clan.

BAIRD

Badge: An eagle's head, with the Latin motto *Dominus fecit* (The Lord made it). Gaelic: *Mac a 'Bhaird* (Son of the bard or poet).

Early in the thirteenth century a Baird was given the estates of Kype in Lanarkshire by William the Lion for saving the king's life from a wild boar, while Robert Baird was granted the barony of Cambusnethan by King Robert Bruce and descendants acquired lands in Banffshire and Aberdeenshire. Famous Bairds include General Sir David (1757–1829), hero of wars in India and the Peninsular campaign, and John Logie Baird, the inventor of television.

BARCLAY

Badge: A hand holding a dagger, with the Latin motto *Aut agere aut mori* (Action or death).

The progenitor of this clan was a Norman named Walter de Berkeley, one of the officials recruited by King David I to reorganize the administration of the kingdom, but the present form of the name first appears in the late fourteenth century. The name is prevalent in Kincardineshire, Aberdeenshire, and Fife. Clansmen include James Barclay of Urie, who became a prominent London banker. From the Barclays of Towie in Aberdeenshire came Field Marshal Prince Michael Barclay de Tolly, ennobled by the Tsar for helping to rid Russia of Napoleon.

BRODIE

Badge: A hand holding three arrows, with the motto "Unite."
Gaelic: *Brothaigh.*

This clan takes its name from a district in Moray. Michael, Thane of Brodie, was ennobled by King Robert Bruce in 1312, although Brodie Castle has been the family seat since the eleventh century. The clan chief has the distinction of being the head of one of the oldest untitled families, and is known as Brodie of Brodie or just Brodie without prefix. Alexander Brodie of Brodie (1617–79) negotiated the Restoration of Charles II (1660), while his grandson of the same name was Lord Lyon King of Arms (1727–54). The most notorious Brodie was the Edinburgh Deacon, allegedly the model for Stevenson's Dr. Jekyll and Mr. Hyde.

BRUCE

Badge: A lion statant with tail extended, with the Latin motto *Fuimus* (We have been).
Gaelic: *Brus.*

Although the name Brus was common among the Vikings of the northern and western isles, this clan derives from the powerful family which came to Scotland, via Normandy and England, in the reign of David I, and had extensive estates in Essex and Yorkshire as well as Annandale and Carrick. Robert Bruce, Lord of Annandale and Earl of Carrick (1274–1329), renewed the struggle for independence in 1306 and decisively defeated the English at Bannockburn. Descendants include the Earls of Elgin, Sir Michael Bruce (author of *Tramp Royal*) and his brother, the actor Nigel Bruce, best remembered for his part as Dr. Watson to Basil Rathbone's Sherlock Holmes.

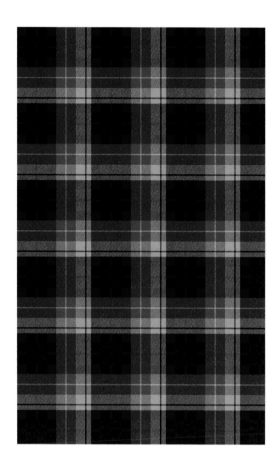

BUCHANAN

Badge: A right hand holding a ducal coronet, with the Latin motto *Audaces juvo* (I prefer the brave).
Gaelic: *Canonach*.

Auslan or Absalon O Kyan, a prince of Ulster, settled in Argyll about 1016 and for his services against the Danes at Clontarf he was granted the lands of *Both-chanain* (canon's seat) east of Loch Lomond. The estate remained in the family's hands until 1682, but other branches held extensive lands in Stirlingshire and Dunbartonshire. Famous clansmen include George Buchanan (1506–82), the foremost Latin scholar of his day and tutor to Mary Queen of Scots, Andrew Buchanan, the Tobacco Lord who laid out Glasgow's smartest shopping street, and James Buchanan, fifteenth President of the United States.

Left: Clatteringshaws Loch was formed by damming the Blackwater of Dee. This is in Bruce territory.

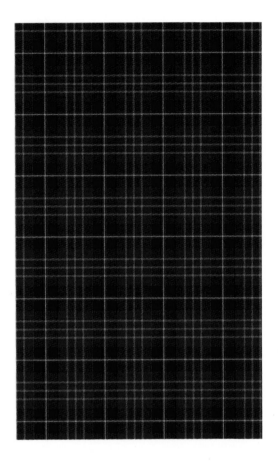

CAMERON

Badge: An arm in armor, the hand holding a sword, with the Latin motto *Pro rege et patria* (For king and country).

Gaelic: *Camshron* (Crooked nose).

One of the oldest clans of Scotland, they have occupied lands in Lochaber since the late thirteenth century, if not earlier. Within this large clan there are several important branches, each with its own badge and tartan, noted separately, although they spring from a common source. By the fifteenth century the most powerful branches of the clan were the MacMartins of Letterfinlay, the MacGillonies of Strone, and the MacSorleys of Glen Nevis. The clan was allied to the Lord of the Isles and fought under his banner at Harlaw in 1411, but later they broke away.

CAMERON OF ERRACHT

Badge: St. Andrew holding his saltire cross.

Gaelic: *Camshron* (Crooked nose).

This important branch of the clan Cameron is derived from Ewen, son of Ewen the clan chief and his second wife Marjory Mackintosh early in the sixteenth century. Donald Cameron of Erracht was a staunch supporter of Prince Charles but fled into exile after Culloden. His son Allan served in the American War of Independence and in 1793 raised the Cameron Highlanders for service in the French Revolutionary War. As the 79th Foot, the regiment has had a long and honorable history in the British Army.

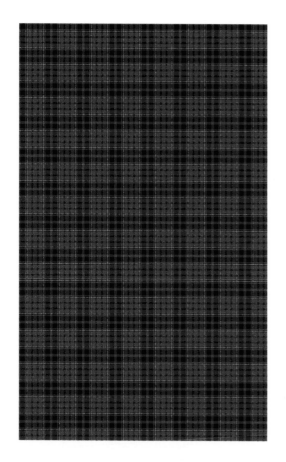

CAMERON OF LOCHEIL

Badge: Five arrows bound together, with the Gaelic motto *Aonaibh ri cheile* (joined to one another).
Gaelic: *Camshron* (Crooked nose).

This major branch of the Camerons traces its descent from the MacGillonies of Strone, later strengthened by intermarriage with the MacMartins of Letterfinlay. By 1528 Cameron of Locheil had emerged as Captain of Clan Cameron and was named as such in a charter from James V. Achnacarry, the clan seat since the seventeenth century, was destroyed by the Duke of Cumberland in 1746 but rebuilt 1802–37. During World War II was an an important Commando training base.

CAMPBELL

Badge: A boar's head, with the Latin motto *Ne obliviscaris* (Do not forget).
Gaelic: *Caimbeul* (Wry-mouth).

This powerful clan traces its origins to Malcolm MacDiarmid, who married a Norman heiress named Beauchamp early in the eleventh century. Their son, Archibald, came to England with the Conqueror in 1066 and was the progenitor of the Beauchamp and Beecham families. The name, meaning "beautiful field" was rendered in medieval Latin as **Campobello**, and from this came Kemble and Campbell. Colin Campbell of Lochow, knighted in 1280, founded the Argyll clan whose spectacular rise is charted in the fortunes of its chiefs, raised to the peerage (1445), given an earldom (1457), a marquessate (1641), and finally a dukedom (1690).

Left: Innischonnell
Castle, the original
stronghold of the
Campbells of Lochawe.

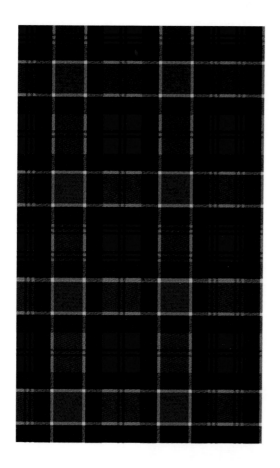

CAMPBELL OF BREADALBANE

Badge: A boar's head, with the motto "Follow me."
Gaelic: *Caimbeul* (Wry-mouth).

This branch of the clan originated with Sir Colin Campbell of Lochow who acquired lands in Lorne by marriage, built Kilchurn Castle, and distinguished himself in the Crusades. His descendants extended their lands in Argyll and Perthshire by judicious marriages. Sir John Campbell was created Earl of Breadalbane in 1681 and this title became a marquessate of the United Kingdom peerage in 1831, but the death of John, fifth Earl, in 1862 brought this title to an end. It was conferred on Gavin, seventh Earl, in 1885, but he died without issue in 1922 and it has been defunct ever since.

CAMPBELL OF CAWDOR

Badge: A crowned swan, with the motto "Be mindful."
Gaelic: *Caimbeul* (Wry-mouth).

In 1510 Sir John Campbell, third son of the second Earl of Argyll, married Muriel, daughter of Sir John Calder of Calder in Nairnshire, through whom the ancient title of Thane of Cawdor (once borne by Macbeth) passed to their grandson John Campbell. Marriage with a Pryce heiress in the eighteenth century brought extensive estates in Pembrokeshire. John Campbell, created Baron Cawdor in 1796, is remembered for defeating the French at Fishguard in 1797, the last foreign invasion of British soil. His son was created Earl Cawdor in 1827, taking the courtesy title of Viscount Emlyn from his Welsh estates. The impressive Cawdor Castle dates from 1454, although parts of it are undoubtedly much older.

Left: Cawdor Castle.

Far Left: Kilchurn Castle, built by the Campbells of Breadalbane.

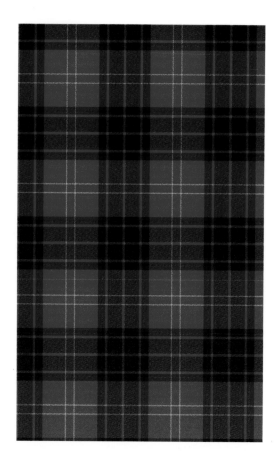

CHISHOLM

Badge: A boar's head impaled on a hand-held dagger, with the Latin motto *Feros ferio* (I strike the fierce).
Gaelic: *Siosal.*

Although this clan is firmly associated with the Highlands, with lands in Erchless and Strathglass, it is actually of Norman origin and derives its name from Chesilholm (gravel holm) in Roxburghshire. The family held lands in Berwickshire, but the move north came in the late-twelfth century when a Chisholm became Thane of Caithness. Sir Robert Chisholm became constable of Urqhuart Castle on Loch Ness in 1359 and his son Alexander married the heiress of Erchless, which has been the clan seat ever since. The Chisholms were ardent Jacobites, successive chiefs distinguishing themselves at Sheriffmuir (1715) and Culloden (1746).

CLAN CHATTAN

Badge: A cat salient with the motto "Touch not the cat bot [without] a glove."
Gaelic: *Clann Gillechatan.*

This is a super-clan or confederation of clans, the individual members of which have as their emblem a cat in various guises. The Clan of the Cats was a close alliance in the north of Scotland as far back as the late twelfth century, and eventually comprised the Davidsons, Farquharsons, Mackintoshes, Macphersons, Macgillivrays, and Macbeans. The first chief was the eleventh-century Gillechattan Mor, whose descendant Eva married Angus, sixth Laird of Macintosh, Captain of Clan Chattan. His claim to the chiefship was contested by the chief of the clan Macpherson and this led to a long-running feud between the Mackintoshes and the Macphersons which rumbles on to this day.

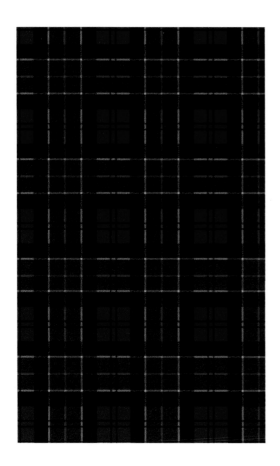

COLQUHOUN

Badge: A hart's head, with the French motto *Si je puis* (If I can).

Gaelic: *Mac a'Chombaich*.

The clan takes its name from Colquhoun (pronounced "Cohoon") in Dunbartonshire, granted to Humphrey of Kilpatrick in the early thirteenth century. Subsequently, the estate of Luss on Loch Lomond was added by marriage. A feud between the Colquhouns and the Macgregors came to a head in 1603 when an attempt by Colquhouns to ambush their enemies was forestalled. In the resulting battle at Glenfruin, the last armed confrontation between rival clans on the Scottish mainland, the Colquhouns were soundly beaten and their chief killed. As a result of charges laid against the Macgregors that clan was proscribed, its lands seized, and even the very name expunged.

Left: Loch Lomond seen from Luss.

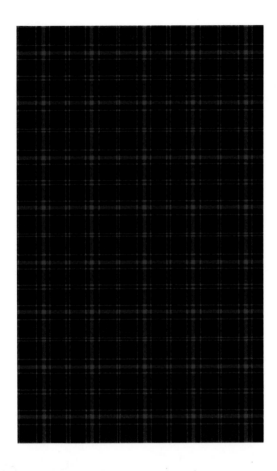

CUMMING

Badge: A lion rampant holding a dagger, with the motto "Courage."
Gaelic: *Cuimean.*

The clan is descended from the Cumins or Comyns (both forms are still in use), a powerful family in Badenoch whose progenitor was Robert de Comyn, governor of Northumberland after the Conquest, whose grandson William was appointed Chancellor of Scotland by David I. Originally the Comyns held lands in Roxburghshire, but by marriage they acquired estates in Badenoch and Buchan. The Black Comyn, one of the Guardians of Scotland in the 1290s, backed John Baliol and thus fell foul of Robert Bruce. His son John was stabbed to death by Bruce at Dumfries in 1306, the foul deed which triggered off the War of Independence. Famous clansmen include the big-game hunter Roualeyn Gordon-Cumming and the actors Robert Cumming and Peggy Cummins.

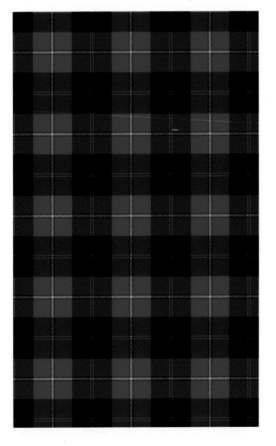

CUNNINGHAM

Badge: A unicorn's head, with the motto "Over fork over."
Gaelic: *MacCuinneagain.*

This family is of Norman origin and derives its name from the district of Cunningham, one of the ancient baileries of Ayrshire. It was well established there in the mid-twelfth century but came to prominence at the Battle of Largs in 1263. By marriage the chief acquired the lands of Glencairn from which his descendant took his title when created an earl in 1488. The Y-shaped device on the arms of Marquess Conyngham (used as the emblem of Cunninghame district) and the motto allude to an incident during the War of Independence when Robert Bruce was concealed from his pursuers by a Cunningham who forked straw over him as he lay in a cowshed. The fourteenth Earl was the patron of Robert Burns, immortalized in a lament of 1791. With the death of the fifteenth Earl five years later the earldom became extinct. Famous clansmen include Robert "Don Roberto" Cunningham-Graham and the World War II naval commander Viscount Cunningham.

DAVIDSON

Badge: A stag's head with the Latin motto *Sapienter si sincere* (Wisely if sincerely).
Gaelic: *MacDhaibhidh*.

Because the pronunciation of the Gaelic name (in which the aspirated consonants are silent) sounds rather like Mackay, there is an erroneous assumption that the two clans are connected. The progenitor of this clan was Black David of Invernahaven, fourth son of Muireach, Parson of Kingussie (1173), who founded the clan Macpherson. From the founding father the clan came to be known as Clan Dhai, Anglicized as Davidson. Intermarriage with the rival Mackintosh clan brought the Davidsons into the Clan Chattan confederacy in the early fourteenth century. The Davidsons became embroiled in the feud between the Macphersons and Mackintoshes, and in the battle at the North Inch of Perth (1396), when thirty picked men on either side fought to the death, only one Davidson escaped with his life, by swimming across the River Tay.

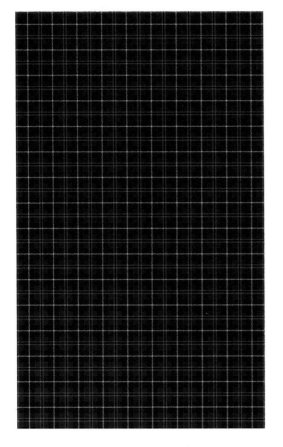

DOUGLAS

Badge: A salamander amid flames, on top of a cap of maintenance, with the French motto *Jamais arrière* (Never behind).
Gaelic: *Dubhghlas*.

This powerful clan takes its name from a place in southern Lanarkshire meaning "black stream" and came to prominence during the War of Independence when the Black Douglas was Bruce's chief supporter. Over the ensuing centuries the fortunes of this family have ebbed and flowed, marrying into the royal family a dozen times and holding the chief offices of state. From the Douglases stem the earls, marquesses, and dukes of Queensberry, the earls of Morton, and the dukes of Douglas, although, as a result of deaths without issue, some of these titles passed to the Dukes of Buccleuch and Hamilton. Most notorious of the Queensberry branch were the second Duke, who engineered the Union of 1707, the celebrated rake, known as "Old Q," the Marquess who devised the rules of boxing, and his younger son Lord Alfred Douglas, the "Bosie," who played a shameful part in the downfall of Oscar Wilde.

Right: Tantallon Castle, and Bass Rock, Lothian, in Douglas territory.

DRUMMOND

Badge: A goshawk, with the motto "Gang warily."
Gaelic: *Drummann*.

The clan takes its name from Drymen near Loch Lomond in Dunbartonshire and traces its roots back to Maurice, Prince of Hungary, who escorted to Scotland Princess Margaret, the future wife of Malcolm Canmore. Malcolm de Drymen supported Robert Bruce and is credited with the use of calthrops, the concealed spikes that crippled the English cavalry in the Bruce's battles. He was rewarded with estates in Perthshire. Successive Drummonds served the monarchy well and acquired many titles, including the earldom of Melfort and viscountcy of Strathallan. The senior line became Dukes of Perth, a title forfeited after Culloden.

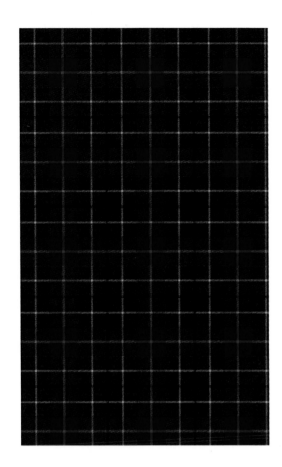

DUNCAN

Badge: A three-masted sailing ship, with the Latin motto *Disce pati* (Learn to suffer).
Gaelic: *Donnachaidh*.

Originally a branch of the Robertsons, the clan traces its origins back to *Donnachadh Reamhar* (Fat Duncan) who led the clan at Bannockburn and tipped the balance in favor of Bruce. In later times the Duncans held lands in Angus. Sir William Duncan was a physician to George III and created a baronet, but the most illustrious member of the family was Adam Duncan, who rose through the ranks of the Royal Navy and was created a viscount in recognition of his spectacular victory over the French and Dutch at Camperdown in 1797.

ELLIOT

Badge: An armed fist holding a broadsword, with the Latin motto *Braviter et recte* (Bravely and justly).

Originally this clan was based in Forfar, although whether it derived its name from Eliot, or gave its name to it, is debatable, one school of thought maintaining that the name comes from the Hebrew Elias. About 1395 the clan was persuaded to move to the Borders to defend Liddesdale from English incursions. Like the Armstrongs, they became one of the most powerful of the Border clans. Illustrious members of the clan include George Elliot of Stobs, who became governor of Gibraltar and withstood the four-year siege by France and Spain (1779–83), for which he was raised to the peerage as Lord Heathfield, Baron Gibraltar in 1787. Gilbert Elliot was convicted of high treason (1685) but later pardoned and became Lord Minto in 1705. His great-grandson was Governor-General of India and created Earl of Minto in 1813. His aunt, Jane Elliot, composed the beautiful song "The Flowers of the Forest."

ERSKINE

Badge: A demi-lion rampant, with the Latin motto *Decori decus addit avito* (He adds honor to that of his ancestors).
Gaelic: *Arascain.*

This clan takes its name from the barony of Erskine in Renfrewshire. Closely allied to Robert Bruce by marriage, Sir Robert de Erskine was Great Chamberlain of Scotland. From him are descended the Earls of Mar, Kellie, Buchan, and Rosslyn, whose ranks included the eleventh Earl of Mar, forfeited for his part in the Jacobite Rebellion of 1715, the poetic Earl of Buchan (a contemporary of Burns), and Thomas, Lord Erskine, who became Lord Chancellor. A brother of the Earl of Mar was Lord Grange, who had his wife Rachel abducted and marooned on the remote island of St. Kilda for several years, to prevent her from exposing a Jacobite plot.

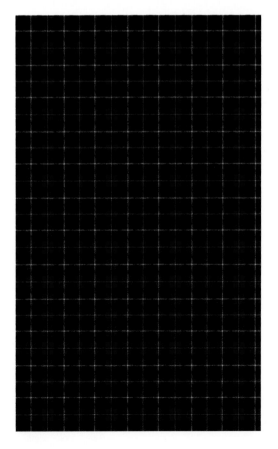

FARQUHARSON

Badge: A demi-lion rampant holding a sword, with the Latin motto *Fide et Fortitudine* (By faith and fortitude).
Gaelic: *MacFhearchair.*

This Aberdeenshire clan takes its name from Farquhar, son of Shaw Mackintosh of Rothiemurchus, who received the forfeited Comyn lands in Braemar from Robert Bruce. Finlay Mor carried the royal standard at Pinkie (1547). Ardent supporters of the Stewarts, the Farquharsons fought at Worcester (1651) and Preston (1715) as well as Falkirk and Culloden during the last Jacobite rebellion. Anne Farquharson of Invercauld, known as "Colonel Anne," mobilized the Mackintoshes for Prince Charlie while her husband fought on the opposing side.

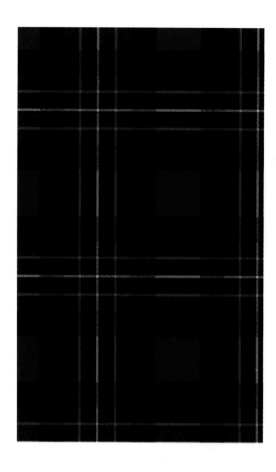

FERGUSON

Badge: A crowned lion rampant issuing from a crown, with the Gaelic motto *Clann Fhearguis gu brath* (Clan Fergus for ever).
Gaelic: *MacFhearghuis.*

As Fergus is a common name, it is probable that the people bearing this surname or variants of it such as Fergus, Ferghie, Macfergus, and Fergusson, now widespread throughout Scotland, come from different roots. Families of this name held lands in Aberdeenshire (Kinmundy and Pitfour), Argyll (Strachur), Perthshire (Dunfallandy and Balquhidder), Fife (Raith), Dumfries-shire (Craigdrarroch), and Ayrshire (Kilkerran). The Craigdarroch branch traces its origins to Fergus, Prince of Galloway, in the twelfth century. Famous clansmen include the ill-starred poet Robert Fergusson. The Kilkerran Fergusons have a long tradition of public service, producing several Lords of Session as well as Sir Bernard Ferguson, who crowned his military career by becoming Governor-General of New Zealand.

Right: Threave Castle, Dumfries & Galloway, in the clan area of the Fergusons.

FLETCHER

Badge: A demi-lion holding a cross, with the Latin motto *Libertate extincta nulla virtus* (Where liberty is dead there is no valor).
Gaelic: *Mac an Fhleisteir.*

This clan is unusual in that its name is derived from a trade, the manufacture of arrows (from the French word *flèche*). Traditionally the Fletchers were closely associated with the Campbells of Argyll and claimed to have been the original inhabitants of Glenorchy. The Fletchers of Glenlyon, on the other hand, were arrowmakers to Clan Gregor, while other important families of this name were the Fletchers of Dunans and the Fletchers of Innerpeffer, Angus. The last named acquired Saltoun in 1643 and their most famous son was Andrew Fletcher (1653–1716), the patriot who led the opposition to the Union in 1707.

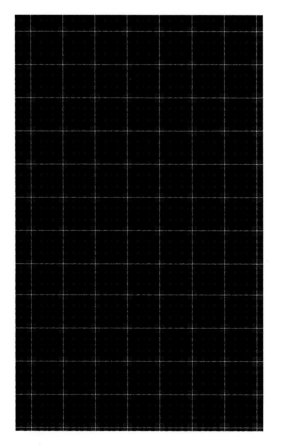

FORBES

Badge: A stag's head, with the motto "Grace me guide."
Gaelic: *Foirbeis.*

The progenitor of this clan was Duncan of Forbes who held the lands of that name in Aberdeenshire from Alexander III in the thirteenth century. His son Alexander was killed at the siege of Urquhart Castle in 1304, while his son Alexander was slain at Dupplin Moor in 1332. A much later Alexander, Lord Pitsligo, opposed the Union and fought in the rebellions of 1715 and 1745 for which his estates were forfeited. Most famous of the family was Duncan Forbes of Culloden, Lord President at the time of the "Forty-five," who persuaded many of the clans not to support the Stewart cause. In Scotland generally the name is pronounced "Forbs" but in Aberdeenshire it is pronounced "Forb-es." Orville Fawbus was a clansman.

FRASER

Badge: A buck's head, with the French motto *Je suis prest* (I am ready).
Gaelic: *Friseal.*

The clan originated with a Norman mercenary whose name was either Fraise (strawberry) or Fraisier (strawberry plant). He settled in Tweeddale late in the eleventh century during the reign of Malcolm Canmore and had extensive estates in the Borders. Sir Andrew Fraser acquired the Lovat estates through marriage with a daughter of the Earl of Orkney. Simon Fraser, Lord Lovat, was "out" in 1715, but executed after the 1745–46 rebellion. His descendant raised the Lovat Scouts which saw service in the Boer War and later British conflicts. Other clansmen include Simon Fraser, who explored the Fraser River in Canada, and Peter Fraser (1884–1950), prime minister of New Zealand (1940–49).

Right: Heather in bloom in Glen Convinth near Loch Ness—Fraser territory.

GORDON

Badge: A buck's head, with the Lowland Scots motto *Bydand* (Remaining).
Gaelic: *Gordon.*

This powerful northern clan originated in the Borders, deriving its name from
Gordon in Berwickshire where a Norman progenitor held lands of David I. Sir
Adam de Gordon undertook a diplomatic mission to the Pope in 1320, bearing a
copy of the Declaration of Arbroath, and was rewarded by Robert Bruce with lands
in Strathbogie. His descendant was created Earl of Huntly in 1449, and this became
successively a marquessate (1599) and a dukedom (1684). In 1794 Jane, Duchess of
Gordon, raised a regiment for the French war, rewarding each recruit with a kiss.
Famous clansmen include George Gordon, Lord Byron, and General Charles
"Chinese" Gordon, the heroic defender of Khartoum.

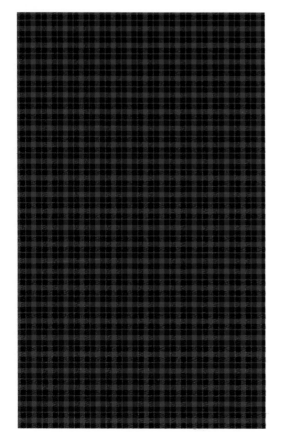

GOW

Badge: A thistle, with the Latin motto *Juncta arma decori* (Arms united to glory).
Gaelic: *Mac a'Ghobhainn* (son of the smith).

As a trade surname Gow is associated with several other clans, notably the
Macphersons, as a result of the blacksmith Hal o' the Wynd agreeing to make up
the number of that clan at the battle of the North Inch in 1396. The Gows were
chiefly to be found in Inverness-shire and Perthshire, and included the celebrated
fiddlers Neil (1727–1807) and his son Nathaniel (1766–1831). The Macgowans,
sometimes regarded as a separate clan, are mainly found in the central Lowlands
and Dumfries-shire.

GRAHAM

Badge: An eagle preying on a stork, with the French motto *N'oubliez* (Do not forget).
Gaelic: *Greumach.*

One of the oldest clans, the name was well established by the early twelfth century when David I granted lands to William de Graham in Lothian. Grahams have played a prominent part in Scottish military history, from Sir John, killed under Wallace at Falkirk (1298), to Thomas, Lord Lynedoch (1750–1843), a hero of the Peninsular War. In between came Earls, Marquesses, and Dukes of Montrose, including the Great Marquess (executed in 1650) and the third Duke who was responsible for the repeal of the legislation prohibiting Highland dress. The present duke, long resident in Zimbabwe, was a leading supporter of Ian Smith's government. The clan also include John Graham of Claverhouse, Viscount Dundee, killed in the moment of victory at Killiecrankie (1689), and the celebrated American evangelist, Dr. Billy Graham.

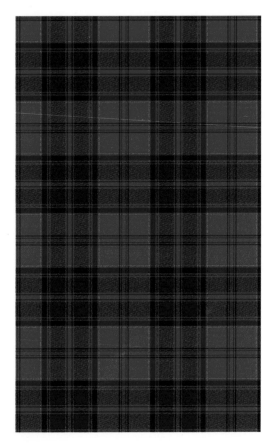

GRANT

Badge: An inflamed mountain, with the motto "Stand fast."
Gaelic: *Grannd.*

Although it is sometimes asserted that the name derives from the Gaelic word *granda* (ugly), it is pure French, meaning "large" or "eminent," and testifies to the Norman origin of the clan where the French equivalent of the motto "Stand fast" was in use before 1066. It may be that a scion of this family married a *Siol Alpin* (the seed of Alpin) heiress who could trace her roots back to the tenth century, but in Scotland the Grants first appear as sheriffs of Inverness in the thirteenth century. Lawrence Grant married a Comyn heiress and thus acquired Strathspey, the district most associated with the clan to this day. Ulysses S. Grant, commander of the Union armies in the American Civil war and seventeenth President (1868–76) is probably the most famous clansman, although the French composer Bizet was descended from a Bisset, a sept of the clan.

GUNN

Badge: A right hand wielding a broadsword, with the Latin motto *Aut pax aut bellum* (Either peace or war).
Gaelic: *Guinne*.

Although this clan claims descent from Gunni, son of Olaf the Black, Norse King of Man and the Isles in the twelfth century, it is now believed that it is derived from a Pictish tribe inhabiting Caithness a thousand years earlier. Extremely warlike and unruly, the clan was forced to migrate southward and resettle in Sutherland in the fifteenth century. George Gunn the Crowner (a hereditary legal appointment) was the father of many sons, each of whom was the progenitor of families which are now septs of the clan.

HAMILTON

Badge: An oak tree on a ducal coronet, with the motto "Through."
Gaelic: *Hamultun*.

Like the Barclays, this clan derives its name from a place in England—Hambledon in the Thames Valley—which the Norman progenitor held of the Conqueror. Half a century later, the first of the family to head north arrived in Scotland and from him was descended Walter Fitz Gilbert, governor of Bothwell Castle at the end of the thirteenth century. Changing sides, he was rewarded by Robert Bruce with the barony of Cadzow in Lanarkshire, from which the Hamilton estates expanded in the ensuing centuries. James, sixth of Cadzow, was created Lord Hamilton in 1445, but his son James became Earl of Arran in 1503 and Duke of Chatelherault (France) in 1549. Eventually the head of this powerful family held three dukedoms, adding Hamilton (1643) and Brandon in England. A grandson of the second Earl of Arran became Earl of Abercorn (1606) and descendants became Marquess (1790) and Duke (1868). From a junior branch spring the Earls of Haddington.

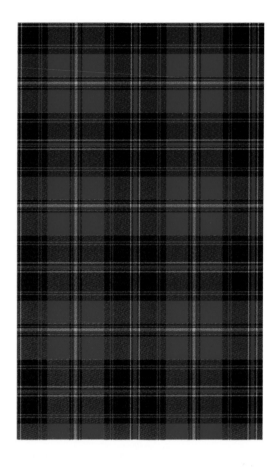

HAY

Badge: A falcon with outstretched wings, with the Latin motto *Serva jugum* (Save the yoke).
Gaelic: *Mac Garaidh.*

Another of the Norman families which came to Scotland in the twelfth century, the Hays trace their origins to William de la Haye, cup-bearer to Malcolm IV. His eldest son, William, was the progenitor of the Earls of Errol while his second son Robert was the ancestor of the Hays of Yester who later gained the marquessate of Tweeddale. In 1314 Gilbert de la Haye was confirmed as hereditary High Constable of Scotland under Robert Bruce and this office has ever since been held by successive Earls of Errol, taking precedence over all other hereditary honors after the Blood Royal. The Earls of Kinnoul are an offshoot from the Hays of Errol. The name comes from the French word *hail* (hedge), hence the Gaelic equivalent *garadh.*

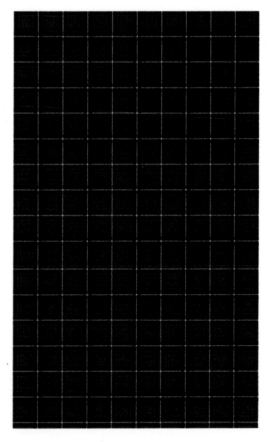

HENDERSON

Badge: A hand holding a five-pointed star surmounted by a crescent, with the Latin motto *Sola virtus nobilitat* (Valor alone ennobles).
Gaelic: *Mac Eanruig.*

This name, meaning son of Henry, gives rise to such variants as Henryson, Hendry, and Mackendrick, found in many parts of Scotland. Another variant, Eanrick, is regarded as a sept of clan Gunn, descended from Henry, son of George the Crowner. The main clan, however, originated in Glencoe. A daughter of the Henderson chief married Iain Macdonald, brother of the first Lord of the Isles, and from them were descended the Maclain Macdonalds of Glencoe, massacred by the Campbells in 1692. Alexander Henderson (1583–1646) was a celebrated churchman who drafted the National Covenant (1638) and the Solemn League and Covenant (1643). More recent clansmen have included the actor Ian Hendry and the film director Sandy Mackendrick.

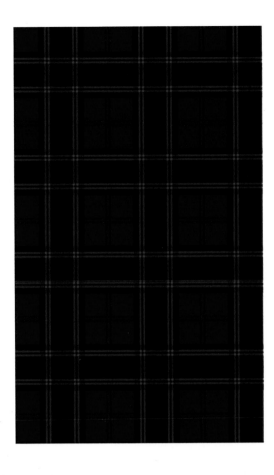

HOME

Badge: A lion's head on a cap of maintenance, with the motto "A Home, A Home, A Home."

Gaelic: *Uamh* (cave).

This name is pronounced "Hume" (and often thus spelled) and derives from a place in Berwickshire which was settled by descendants of Earl Gospatrick of Northumbria in the thirteenth century. By marriage and clan foray the Homes became one of the most powerful Border families. Distinguished clansmen include the Earls of Home, the philosopher David Hume (1711–76), and the playwright John Home, whose patriotic drama *Douglas* (1756) provoked a member of the first-night audience to cry out rhetorically, "Whaur's yer Wullie Shakespeare noo?" The fourteenth Earl renounced his title and, as Sir Alec Douglas-Home, was British Prime Minister in 1963–64, but later returned to the House of Lords as Baron Home of the Hirsel.

INNES

Badge: A boar's head with the Scots motto "Be traist."

Gaelic: *Inis*.

This clan traces its ancestry to Berowald, a Flemish mercenary in the service of Malcolm IV from whom he received the lands of Innes in Moray in 1154. Berowald's grandson took Innes as his surname and was confirmed in his estates by Alexander II in 1226. The Gaelic word *inis* from which the name is derived merely means an islet (Anglicized as "inch"). Sir Robert Innes acquired the estates of Aberchirder by marriage in the fourteenth century, while his descendant of the same name received a baronetcy from James VI in 1625. Following the death of the fourth Duke of Roxburghe without issue, Sir James Innes in 1812 successfully petitioned the House of Lords for the Scottish titles and lands, and became fifth Duke. James, the sixth Duke, was created Earl Innes in 1838. A cadet branch, the Inneses of Innermarkie, acquired a baronetcy from Charles I in 1631 for services to the Stewart cause.

JOHNSTON

Badge: A phoenix rising from the flames, with the Latin motto *Vive ut postia vivas* (Live that you may live hereafter).
Gaelic: *Maclain*.

The name of this powerful Border clan comes from John's toun, the fortified dwelling of the chief who held lands in Annandale under the forebears of King Robert Bruce. Staunch supporters of the crown, they rose steadily up the social scale. Sir James Johnston was raised to the peerage in 1631 as Lord Johnston of Lochwood, and promoted a decade later to Earl of Hartfell. The second Earl became Earl of Annandale in 1672, and his son became Marquess in 1701. The title became dormant in 1792, but Patrick Hope-Johnston of Westerhall successfully petitioned in 1986 for the revival of the title of Earl of Annandale and Hartfell. The Johnstons of Westerhall were descended from the same stock and became baronets of Nova Scotia in 1700.

KEITH

Badge: A stag's head, with the Latin motto *Veritas vincit* (Truth conquers).
Gaelic: *Ceiteach*.

This important branch of Clan Chattan takes its name from Keith in Banffshire. A fourteenth century marriage of the chief to the heiress of the Cheynes of Ackergill gave the Keiths extensive estates in Caithness, although this brought them into a long-running conflict with the Gunns. The clan chief was hereditary Grand Marischal of Scotland, the fifth Earl Marischal founding the university college of that name in Aberdeen. The tenth Earl was one of the leaders of the 1715 Jacobite Rebellion and was attainted as a result. His brother James had a brilliant career in the army of the Tsar before reorganizing the Prussian army and becoming a field marshal under Frederick the Great.

Left: The impressive
Keith stronghold of
Dunnottar Castle.

KENNEDY

Badge: A swimming dolphin, with the French motto *Avise la fin* (Consider the end).
Gaelic: *Ceannaideach* (ugly head).

Although the Gaelic name simply means "ugly head" it has been suggested that it is actually derived from *cinneadh* (kinsman), alluding to the fact that the progenitor of the clan, Henry, was a brother of William the Lion. The Kennedys first came to prominence in the late-thirteenth century as supporters of the Bruces against the Comyns, and thus acquired lands of Cassilis in Carrick. The grandson of Mary Kennedy and King Robert III was the first Earl of Cassilis. Archibald, twelfth Earl, was created Marquess of Ailsa in 1831. The outlaw Ulric Kennedy fled from Carrick and settled in Lochaber forming the sept of MacWalrick. Culzean Castle (now a Scottish National Trust property) had close associations with Dwight D. Eisenhower when he was Supreme Commander Allied Forces in World War II. It should be noted that the Irish Kennedys are a completely different tribe.

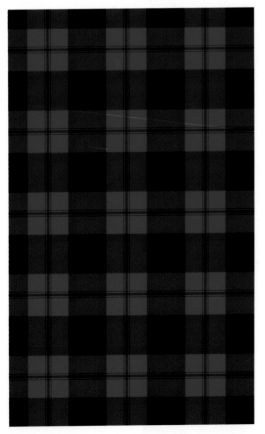

KERR

Badge: A radiate sun, with the Latin motto *Sero sed serio* (Late but serious).
Gaelic: *Cearr* or *MacGhillechearr*.

Two Anglo-Norman brothers who settled in Roxburghshire in the twelfth century were the ancestors of this numerous clan, which, by the fourteenth century, had also established branches in Ayrshire and Aberdeenshire. The Kers of Cessford were wardens of the marches and hereditary sheriffs of Roxburghshire, and from them were descended the Lords, Earls (from 1616), and Dukes (from 1707) of Roxburghe. From a cadet branch, the Kers of Newbattle and Ferniehirst, sprang the Earls of Ancrum and Marquesses of Lothian. The most famous clansman was the actress Deborah Kerr who pronounced her name "car" in the traditional manner.

LAMONT

Badge: An open right hand, with the Latin motto *Ne parcas nec spernas* (Neither spare nor dispose).
Gaelic: *MacLaomainn.*

Rather confusingly, this powerful Argyll clan was at one time known as the Clan Farquhar (MacFhearchair) from an ancestor who lived long before the emergence of the Farquharsons of Aberdeenshire and with whom they had no connection. By the early thirteenth century, however, the chief of the clan had obtained a hereditary judgeship, hence the name "lawman" (*laomann*) from which the present clan name is derived. The Lamonts clashed frequently with the Campbells who massacred over 200 of the clan at Dunoon in 1646. This atrocity was one of the crimes for which the Marquess of Argyll was executed in 1661. The pronunciation of the name, by the way, puts the stress on the first syllable and not the last, as in the "French" style affected by Norman Lamont, the former Chancellor of the Exchequer.

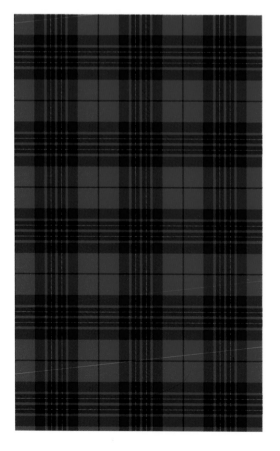

LESLIE

Badge: A demi-griffin, with the motto "Grip fast."
Gaelic: *Mac an Fhleisdeir.*

The name comes from the estate of Leslie in Aberdeenshire which was granted by William the Lion to Malcolm, son of a Flemish noble named Bartholf, in the twelfth century. Conversely, Leslie in Fife takes its name from the family who acquired lands there in the thirteenth century. George Leslie was created Earl of Rothes, raised to a dukedom in 1680. John Leslie, Bishop of Ross, was a leading supporter of Mary Queen of Scots, but the seventeenth century witnessed three Leslies who rose to the highest ranks in the armies of Sweden and the Empire. Alexander Leslie, field marshal under Gustavus Adolphus, became Earl of Leven.

Right: The ruins of Balgonie Castle are in Fife, Leslie territory.

LINDSAY

Badge: A swan rising from a coronet, with the French motto *Endure fort* (Endure bravely).
Gaelic: *MacGhille Fhionnlaigh*.

The name originates from Limesay, Norse for island of lime-trees, a place near Rouen in Normandy. Having come to England with the Conqueror, the first of the family went north in time-honored fashion, Sir Walter de Lindsay receiving the lands of Ercildoun from David I. His grandson, William, married the daughter of Prince Henry of Scotland, and acquired the lands of Crawford in Lanarkshire. David Lindsay married a daughter of Robert II, and was created Earl of Crawford in 1398. The clan has long literary traditions; Sir David Lindsay of the Mount, tutor of James V, wrote *The Three Estaits* (1540) and Robert Lindsay of Pitscottie authored *The Chronicles of Scotland*, while the twenty-sixth Earl was a noted bibliophile.

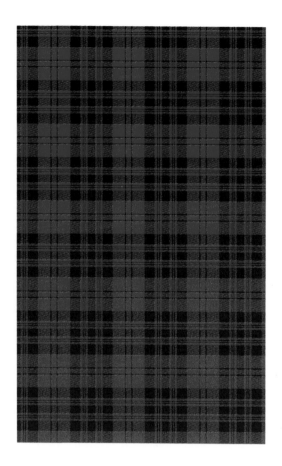

LIVINGSTONE

Badge: A demi-savage, crowned and wreathed with laurels and holding a club and a snake, with the French motto *Si je puis* (If I can).
Gaelic: *Mac an Leigh*.

This is one of the oldest names in Scotland, having been recorded in documents from the eleventh century and derived from the place name Livingston in West Lothian. Sir James Livingston of Callendar was raised to the peerage in 1458. William, fifth Lord Livingston, was guardian of the young Mary, Queen of Scots (ruled 1542–67). Alexander, seventh Lord, was created Earl of Linlithgow in 1600 but the title was forfeited when the fifth Earl was involved in the 1715 rebellion. The Gaelic name, meaning "son of the physician," alludes to the Livingstones of Argyll, a tradition maintained by their most illustrious descendant, Dr. David Livingstone, the missionary-explorer of Africa.

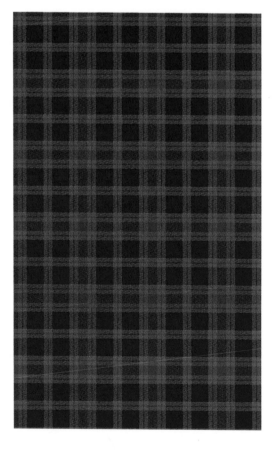

LOGAN

Badge: A heart pieced by a nail, with the Latin motto *Hoc majorum virtus* (This is the valor of my ancestors).
Gaelic: *Loganaich*.

The name of this clan derives from a place and a river (the Logan Water) in Ayrshire, its chiefs being landowners in the southwest of Scotland by the twelfth century. Sir Robert Logan and Sir Walter Logan were named among the followers of the Black Douglas, killed in Spain in 1329 while taking the heart of Robert Bruce to the Holy Land. Sir Robert Logan of Restalrig married a daughter of Robert II and became Admiral of Scotland. The last of the line was outlawed and died in his refuge of Fast Castle, Berwickshire. From the Logans of Drumderfit come the sept of Maclennan. Most famous clansman is Jimmy Logan.

MACALISTER

Badge: A right hand holding a dagger, with the Latin motto *Fortiter* (Boldly).
Gaelic: *MacAlasdair.*

The clan traces its origins to Alexander, son of Donald of Islay and great-grandson of Somerled, Lord of the Isles, who acquired lands in Kintyre. By unwisely allying himself with the Macdougalls of Lorne against Robert Bruce, Alexander forfeited his claim to the Lordship of the Isles. His descendants expanded out of Knapdale, acquiring other estates in Argyll as well as in Arran and Bute. Alexander MacAlister was an ardent Jacobite who fought at Killiecrankie and the Boyne. The MacAlisters of Tarbert were hereditary constables of Tarbert Castle, Loch Fyne.

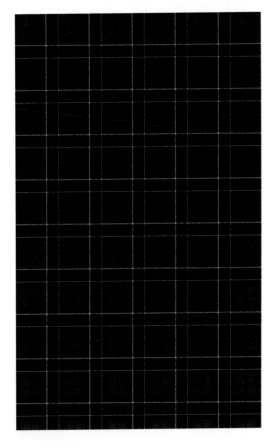

MACALPINE

Badge: A saracen's head dripping blood, with the Gaelic motto *Cuinich bas Alpan* (Remember the death of Alpin).
Gaelic *MacAilpein.*

Paradoxically, although this is undoubtedly one of the oldest names in Scotland, the bearers of this surname were generally regarded as septs of the Grants, Macgregors, Macnabs, or Macaulays, the clans belonging to the confederacy known as **Siol Alpin** (the seed of Alpin). The name goes back to Alpin, King of Scots in the ninth century and father of Kenneth, who became the first King of the Picts and Scots in 843. In more recent times, Robert McAlpine developed one of the country's largest firms of builders and construction engineers and was created baronet in 1918. From him were descended the life peers Baron McAlpine of Moffat and Baron McAlpine of West Green.

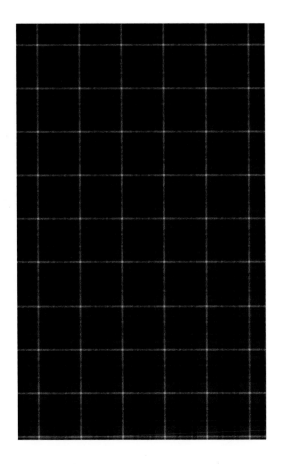

MACARTHUR

Badge: A laurel wreath with the Latin motto *Fide et opera* (By faith and works).
Gaelic: *MacArtair.*

"There is nothing older, unless the hills, MacArthur and the devil" is an old Highland saying, testifying to the antiquity of this clan, although it was, in fact, the senior branch of the Campbells. For their support in the War of Independence, Robert Bruce granted the clan estates in Argyll, including those forfeited from the Macdougalls of Lorne, the clan chief being appointed captain of Dunstaffnage Castle near Oban. After the execution of John Macarthur in 1427, the power of the clan waned. The most famous clansmen are John MacArthur, who introduced merino sheep to Australia, and General Douglas MacArthur, both descended from the MacArthurs of Strachur.

MACAULAY

Badge: An antique boot, with the Latin motto *Dulce periculum* (Peril is sweet).
Gaelic: *MacAmhlaidh.*

The name, meaning son of Olaf, points to a Norse origin for the Macaulays of Lewis who claim descent from Olaf the Black, King of Man and the Isles in the thirteenth century. Branches of this family settled in Sutherland and Wester Ross. They are often regarded as a quite separate clan from the Macaulays of Dunbartonshire who were an offshoot of **Siol Alpin** (the seed of Alpin). The latter trace their descent from Aulay, brother of the Earl of Lennox, in the late thirteenth century, who had his stronghold at Ardincaple near Helensburgh, the clan seat till 1787 when the twelfth chief sold the estate to the Duke of Argyll. The historian Lord Macaulay (1800–59) was a descendant of the Lewis clan, as is the comedian and broadcaster Fred Macaulay of the present day.

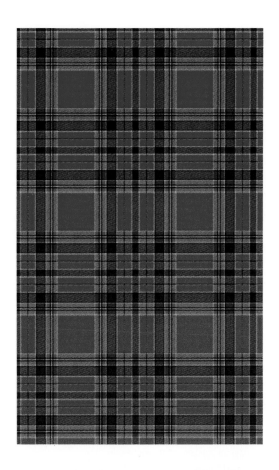

MACBEAN

Badge: A demi-cat rampant with the motto "Touch not the cat bot (without) a glove."
Gaelic: *MacBheathain*.

As its badge and motto indicate, this clan was a branch of the Clan Chattan and derives its name from someone whose epithet means "the fair one," as in Donald Ban, King of Scots in the eleventh century. Claiming descent from Macbeth, the family hailed from Lochaber but moved to Moray in the train of a Clan Chattan heiress, and settled at Kinchyle, Strathnairn, and Dores. Gillies MacBean was one of the heroes of Culloden, killing fourteen Hanoverian soldiers before he was felled. William MacBean enlisted in the army, won the Victoria Cross in the Indian Mutiny, was commissioned, and rose to the rank of major-general.

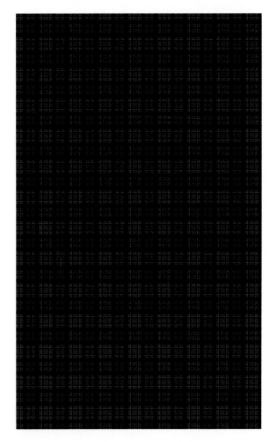

MACCALLUM

Badge: A castle, with the Latin motto *In ardua tendit* (He has attempted difficult things).
Gaelic: *MacChaluim*.

The name signifies a devotee of St. Columba, the Irish saint who converted the Picts to Christianity in the sixth century, and therefore its history is closely connected to the clan Malcolm, hence the similarity of the clan badges and mottoes. The MacCallums held lands at Ariskeodnish, Argyll, but acquired estates at Craignish and Lochavich in the fifteenth century. Dugald MacCallum of Poltalloch adopted the surname Malcolm on succeeding to this estate in 1779. The MacCallums were supporters of the Marquess of Argyll in the wars of the seventeenth century, and renowned for their warlike prowess. Famous clansmen include the actors John and David MacCallum.

MACCOLL

Badge: A six-pointed star within the horns of a crescent, with the Latin motto
Justi ut sidera fulgent (The just shine like stars).
Gaelic: *MacColla.*

The name means son of the high one, and is said to derive from a leading member
of the Clan Donald whose lands were at the head of Loch Fyne, bringing them into
conflict with the Macgregors and the Macphersons. At Drum Nachder in 1602 the
MacColls were slaughtered by their enemies, and thereafter their power and influ-
ence in Argyll waned. Famous clansmen include the Gaelic poet Evan MacColl
(1808–98), whose monument was unveiled at Kenmore in 1930, R.S. McColl, known
as "Toffee Bob" from his confectionery chain, the journalist Ian McColl, a descendant
of the McColls of Mull, and the life peer Lord McColl of Dulwich.

MACDIARMID

Badge: No known badge.
Gaelic: *MacDiarmaid.*

The name is derived from the Old Irish word Diarmait, "a freeman," but first occurs
in Scottish records, somewhat phonetically, as MacTarmayt in 1427. By the middle of
the fifteenth century it was commonly found in various parts of Lorn and Lochaber,
the MacDiarmids being a sept of the Campbells. Alternative spellings are
MacDermot and McDermott. The name is also fairly common in Ireland, the most
famous clansman being John McDermott (Sean MacDiarmada), one of the leaders
of the Easter Rising in 1916 who was executed by the British. On the other hand
Hugh MacDiarmid, Scotland's leading twentieth century poet, was actually
Christopher Murray Grieve, MacDiarmid being only a pen-name.

MACDONALD

Badge: An upright mailed fist holding a cross-crosslet, with the Latin motto *Per mare per terras* (By sea and land).
Gaelic: *MacDhomhnuill*.

By far the greatest, largest, and most prolific of all the Scottish clans, and the commonest surname in Scotland to this day, the Clan Donald traces its Pictish and Norse origins to Donald, grandson of Somerled, King of the Isles. Somerled had married the daughter of Olaf, King of Man, and their three sons were founders of powerful clans such as the Macdougalls of Lorne, as well as the numerous branches of the Macdonalds, noted separately. Nowadays it has become fashionable to speak of Clan Donald in terms of its northern and southern branches, but these have become separate clans with distinctive tartans and variants on the original clan emblem. Among the most prominent clansmen were Sir John Macdonald, Prime Minister of Canada (1867–73 and 1878–91) and Ramsay Macdonald, Prime Minister of Britain (1924 and 1929-35).

Right: Croft at Malacleit on North Uist, part of the Macdonald of the Isles clan area.

MACDONALD OF THE ISLES

Badge: An upright mailed fist holding a cross-crosslet, with the Latin motto *Per mare per terras* (By sea and land).
Gaelic: *MacDhomhnuill.*

Somerled expelled the Norsemen from Arran and Bute in 1135 but himself fell in battle at Renfrew in 1164, when he challenged Malcolm IV. From his son Reginald (Ranald) came Donald of Islay, progenitor of the clan, whose son, Angus, originally supported Haco of Norway. His son, Angus Og (young Angus) atoned for this by supporting Robert Bruce in the War of Independence, and his son John became Lord of the Isles in 1354. Through marriage, Alexander became Earl of Ross. His son John declared his independence but was defeated by James IV, the title Lord of the Isles being abolished in 1493 and his lands given to the Campbells. John himself died without legitimate issue in 1498.

MACDONALD OF SLEAT

Badge: An armored fist holding a cross-crosslet, with the Latin motto *Per mare per terras* (By sea and land).
Gaelic: *MacDhomhnuill.*

The Macdonalds of Sleat in southern Skye spring from Hugh, third son of Alexander, third Lord of the Isles, who died in 1498. In the early years there was a rapid succession of chiefs, either slain in battle or murdered by their nearest and dearest. For centuries the history of this turbulent clan is one of internecine feuding, and it was not until 1610 that Donald Gorm Mor, seventh of Sleat, and other island chiefs agreed to keep the king's peace. His nephew and successor, Sir Donald, was created a baronet of Nova Scotia in 1625, but the fourth baronet, known as Sir Donald of the Wars, lost his lands for participating in the 1715 Rebellion. Alexander, ninth baronet, was raised to the Irish peerage in 1766 as Baron MacDonald of Slate (sic). The present chief, Sir Ian Godfrey Bosville Macdonald of Sleat, is the seventeenth baronet and twenty-fifth chief.

Left: Tioram Castle is in the territory of the Macdonalds of Ardnamurchan. This branch of the clan is often known as MacIan, from John, son of Angus, which had its seat at Mingary in the most westerly peninsula of mainland Scotland and from which they controlled the smaller islands to the north. By the end of the fifteenth century, however, they were in decline, persecuted by their powerful and ruthless Campbell neighbors. In the seventeenth century they took to the seas and earned a certain notoriety for preying on coastal shipping. Dr. Samuel Johnson, on his tour of the Hebrides, was taken aback when a Highland chief asked him if he was one of the Johnsons of Ardnamurchan— actually a sept of the MacIan Macdonalds.

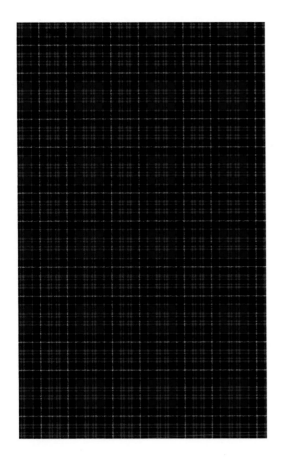

MACDONALD OF CLANRANALD

Badge: A triple-towered castle surmounted by an armored arm holding a sword, with the motto "My hope is constant in thee."
Gaelic: *MacDhomhnuill.*

The clan takes its name from Reginald or Ranald, younger son of John, Lord of the Isles, who obtained lands in the northern Hebrides and mainland in 1373. From this root come the sub-branches of the clan in Moidart, Morar, Knoydart, and Glengarry. A long and bitter feud between the various factions of the Macdonalds was only resolved by the showdown known as *Blar na Leine* (the field of shirts) in 1544, when Macdonald fought Macdonald stripped to the waist. As a result John of Moidart emerged as the victor. Clanranald supported the Stewarts in the wars and rebellions of the seventeenth and eighteenth centuries. Famous clansmen include Flora Macdonald and Etienne Macdonald, Marshal of France and Duke of Taranto.

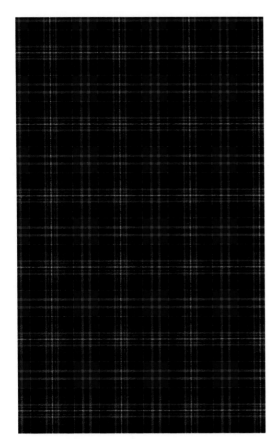

MACDONNELL OF GLENGARRY

Badge: A raven perched on a rock, with the Gaelic motto *Creagan an fhitich* (raven's rock).
Gaelic: *MacDhomhnuill.*

This branch of Clan Donald is descended from Donald, eldest son of Ranald, and is, therefore, a branch of Clanranald. The distinctive spelling of the surname was adopted in the seventeenth century. From Alasdair, fourth chief of Glengarry, the clan takes its Gaelic patronymic of *Mac 'ic Alasdair.* Eneas of Glengarry was one of the earliest supporters of Montrose, forfeited by Cromwell in 1651 but created Lord MacDonell at the restoration. The clan were ardent Jacobites who fought at Killiecrankie and in the rebellions of 1715 and 1745–46. A famous clansman was James MacDonnell, the American aircraft pioneer.

Left: Loch Moidart is in Clanranald territory.

MACDONNELL OF KEPPOCH

Badge: A triple-towered castle surmounted by an armored arm holding a sword, with the motto "My hope is constant in thee."
Gaelic: *MacDhomhnuill.*

Originally a branch of the Clanranald Macdonalds based in Lochaber, this clan traces its origins from Alasdair Carrach, third son of John, first Lord of the Isles and a grandson of Robert II. There was a long-running feud between this clan and the Mackintoshes, largely because the Macdonnells occupied their land by custom, in defiance of a charter which had been granted to the Mackintoshes. Matters came to a head at Blar na Leine in 1544, for his part in which Ranald Macdonnell was executed. Successive chiefs were outlawed but gained distinction in the armies of Sweden and Spain. The Well of the Heads in Invergarry commemorates the beheading of the seven men who murdered the twelfth chief in 1663. The clan struck the first blow in the "Forty-Five," capturing government troops at Glenfinnan before the rebellion commenced.

MACDOUGALL

Badge: A bent right arm in armour, holding a cross-crosslet, with the Latin motto *Vincere et mori* (To win or die).
Gaelic: *MacDhugaill.*

The clan takes its name from Dougal, son of Somerled of the Isles. Dougal's son Duncan received lands in Lorne and his son, Ewin, married a daughter of the Red Comyn murdered by Robert Bruce at Dumfries in 1306. As a result, the Macdougalls were sworn enemies of the Bruce who, fleeing from his enemies, discarded his cloak and a large brooch, ever afterwards known as the Brooch of Lorne and an important clan treasure. Years later a granddaughter of Bruce married the chief but their son John died without issue and his lands passed to the Stewarts of Lorne in 1388. The chiefship later passed to John MacAlan Macdougall of Dunollie. Iain Ciar was forfeited in 1715 but the clan lands were restored in 1745 when it remained loyal to the Hanoverian cause.

Left: Winter sun over

Loch Garry.

MACDUFF

Badge: A demi-lion rampant holding a dagger, with the Latin motto *Deus juvat* (God helps).
Gaelic: *MacDhuibh*.

This name, meaning "son of the dark man" was a patronymic of the Celtic Earls of Fife, the first of whom overthrew Macbeth in 1056 and helped Malcolm Canmore regain the throne. In succeeding generations Macduff had the role of crowning the king. Duncan, Earl of Fife, having allied himself to Edward I, refused to crown Robert Bruce, but his sister Isabel, Countess of Buchan, performed this duty instead. The earldom died out in 1353 but was revived in the eighteenth century. Alexander Duff (1849–1912), Earl of MacDuff and Duke of Fife, founded the British South Africa Company. His wife was Princess Louise, daughter of Edward VII, and their daughter, Princess Alexandra Victoria, married Prince Arthur, Duke of Connaught.

MACEWEN

Badge: The stump of an oak-tree sprouting young branches, with the Latin motto *Reviresco* (I grow green).
Gaelic: *MacEoghainn*.

According to the historian Skene, this clan, with the Macneills and Maclachlans, formed the **Siol Gillivray** (the seed of Gillivray) and was in existence long before 1450, holding lands at Otter on the shores of Loch Fyne where the ancient ruins of MacEwen's Castle can be seen to this day. The progenitor of this clan flourished at the beginning of the thirteenth century, but Swene MacEwen, ninth and last chief, surrendered his lands to Duncan Campbell in 1432. This landless clan was then scattered all over the Highlands and the southwest of Scotland.

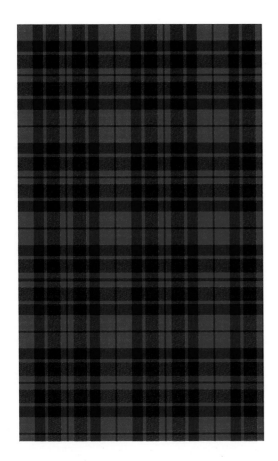

MACFADYEN

Badge: No known badge.

Gaelic: *MacPhaidein.*

The name means "son of little Patrick," and is of Irish origin, the earliest record being of a Padyne Regan living at Dublin in 1264. People of this name were settled in Mull by the beginning of the fourteenth century and among the various spellings recorded thereafter are MacFadyen, MacFadyean, and MacFadzean, the last being probably the commonest form nowadays. The MacFaddens were originally a sept of the MacLeans or MacLaines. Most famous clansmen include Sir Frank (later Lord) MacFadzean, Lord Macfadyen, a Scottish lawlord, and Jean MacFadden, one of Glasgow's most prominent political figures over the past 30 years.

MACFARLANE

Badge: A demi-savage holding a sheaf of arrows and an imperial crown, with the motto "This I'll defend."

Gaelic: *MacPharlain.*

This clan from Loch Lomondside is descended from Gilchrist, brother of the third Earl of Lennox in the thirteenth century. Gilchrist's great-grandson was Bartholomew, rendered in Gaelic as **Parlan**. Duncan, the sixth chief, obtained the estate of Arrochar from the Earl of Lennox in 1395. Intermarriage with the Lennox family brought the Macfarlanes close to the crown in the sixteenth century but at Langside (1567) they were prominent in their opposition to Mary, Queen of Scots. Backing the wrong side in the conflicts of the seventeenth century, the clan was outlawed and many emigrated to Ireland and America (where the present chief resides).

**Left: Dunfermline
Abbey is in Macduff
territory.**

MACFIE or MACPHEE

Badge: A demi-lion rampant, with the Latin motto *Pro rege* (For the king).
Gaelic: *MacDubh-shithe*.

The Gaelic name translates as "dark of peace" and is sometimes rendered phonetically as MacCuish or MacDuffie. Dubhshith was a reader at Iona in 1164, but the origins of this clan are lost in the mists of antiquity and it claimed to belong to *Siol Alpin* (the seed of Alpin). This clan had the distinction of possessing the island of Colonsay, with a burial ground on the tidal islet of Oronsay, but the island passed from their hands in the mid-seventeenth century. As a landless clan, the Macphees were scattered all over Scotland, giving rise to such variants as Cathie, Fee, MacGuffie, and MacHaffie. Ewen Macphee earned notoriety in the nineteenth century as "the last Scottish outlaw." Having deserted from the army he squatted on an island in Loch Quoich, but in old age was evicted for sheep-stealing.

MACGILLIVRAY

Badge: A seated cat, with the motto "Touch not the cat bot (without) a glove."
Gaelic: *MacGhille-brath*.

The Gaelic name, which translates as "son of the servant of judgment," points to an hereditary judgeship enjoyed by the clan's progenitor, but nothing is known for certainty, beyond the fact that it belonged to Clan Chattan and was formerly very numerous in Morven, Lochaber, and Mull. In one of the many upheavals of the late Middle Ages, however, the clan was displaced by one of the royal expeditions against the Highlands and Islands and placed itself under the protection of the Mackintoshes, obtaining lands in Strathnairn. At Culloden Alexander Macgillivray of Dunmaglas led Clan Chattan to victory over the left wing of the Hanoverian army.

MACGREGOR

Badge: A crowned lion's head, with the Gaelic motto *Is rioghail mo dhream* (Royal is my race).
Gaelic: *MacGrioghair*.

The motto alludes to the claim that the clan is descended from Greg MacGraith, an eighth century King of the Picts, recalled in the place names Ecclesgreig and St. Cyrus in Kincardineshire. The earliest references to the clan, however, place it in Glenorchy in the twelfth century. Warlike and unruly, they were harassed and persecuted by their neighbors, and finally proscribed in 1603. This was revoked by Charles II but reapplied by William III and it was not until 1775 that the Macgregors were amnestied. The most famous clansmen are Rob Roy Macgregor (1671–1743) and the Norwegian composer Edvard Grieg whose Scottish grandfather settled in Bergen.

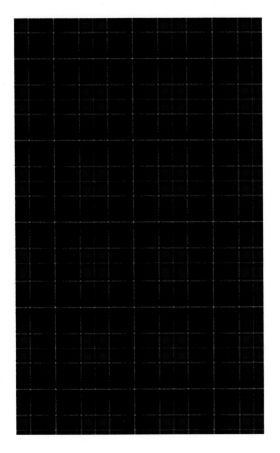

MACINNES

Badge: A bee sucking a thistle, with the Latin motto *E labore dulcedo* (Pleasure comes from work).
Gaelic: *MacAonghais*.

This clan claims to be one of the oldest, although its connection with the Cineal Angus, one of the three tribes of Dalriada in the fifth century, seems doubtful, as the clan had no lands in that district. They first appear in recorded history in the twelfth century, residing in Morven where they were constables of Kinlochaline Castle, overlooking the Sound of Mull, until 1645. The Macinneses were also hereditary archers to Clan Mackinnon, hence the branch of the clan which settled in Skye.

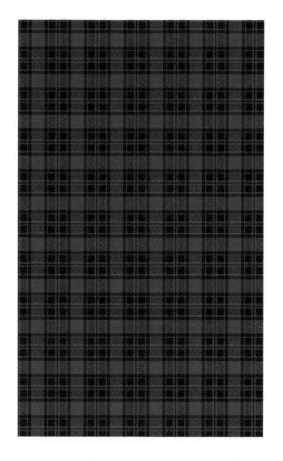

MACINTOSH or MACKINTOSH

Badge: A cat salient, with the motto "Touch not the cat bot (without) a glove."

Gaelic: *Mac an Toisich* (Son of the thane).

The Gaelic name denotes a descent from the senior cadet of a clan, and the Mackintoshes have, indeed, been regarded as one of the most prominent branches of the Clan Chattan for a long time—as a result of the marriage in 1291 of Angus, sixth of Macintosh, to Eva the heiress of Clan Chattan. The rise of this powerful clan, however, was resented by the Earls of Moray and Huntly as well as neighboring clans. Mackintosh chiefs had a rather quirky record, one leading the Covenanters of the North, but another opposing Cromwell, and a third supporting William of Orange. Yet the clan is best remembered for its role in the later Jacobite rebellions. Brigadier Macintosh of Borlum was a Jacobite general in 1715. Thirty years later the Mackintosh served in the Hanoverian army while his wife raised the clan which routed the government forces at Moy.

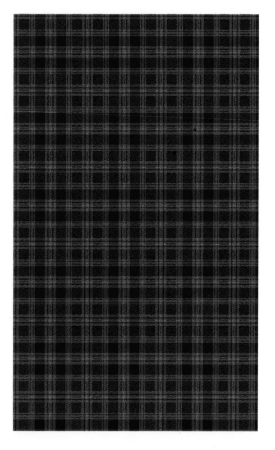

MACINTYRE

Badge: A right hand holding a dagger, with the Latin motto *Per ardua* (through struggles).

Gaelic: *Mac an t-Saoir.*

The name translates as "son of the carpenter," hence the name Wright, which is a sept of the clan, along with Mactear and Mactire. It seems probable that this numerous clan arose from the profession of carpentry, rather than the fanciful explanation that it once held lands in Kintyre, and this explains why it was so wide-spread all over the Highlands. The chief family held lands in Glencoe until 1806 when they were sold, many clansmen them migrating to America. Various branches of the clan held office as hereditary foresters to the Stewarts of Appin, or pipers to Clanranald and Clan Menzies. The most famous clansman is Duncan Macintyre (*Donnachaidh Ban nan Oran*—Fair Duncan of the songs), the celebrated Gaelic poet (1724–1812).

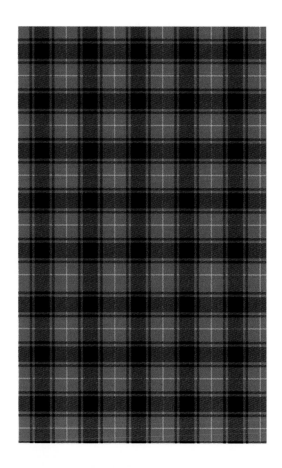

MACIVER

Badge: A boar's head, with the Latin motto *Nunquam obliviscar* (I shall never forget).

Gaelic: *Mac Iomhair*.

Tradition claims that this clan formed part of the expedition of Alexander II which subjugated Argyll in 1221, and received the lands of Glassary as a reward. From there they expanded into Cowal and Lochaber, although later branches also settled in Glenelg. By the sixteenth century the clan had broken up, many clansmen then assuming the name of Campbell, although the name Maciver survived on the isle of Lewis and in the westerly parts of Ross-shire.

MACKAY

Badge: A hand holding a dagger, with the Latin motto *Manu forti* (With a strong hand).

Gaelic: *MacAoidh*.

Known also as Clan Morgan from Morgan, son of Magnus in the early fourteenth century, the clan traces its descent from Morgan's grandson *Aodh* (Hugh) whose mother was a Macneil of Gigha. This large and powerful clan occupied lands in the far northwest of Scotland and was frequently at odds with its neighbors, the Earls of Caithness and Sutherland. Noted for their warlike spirit, they were recruited by Sir Donald Mackay of Farr to serve under Gustavus Adolphus in the Thirty Years' War (1618–48). Sir Donald was raised to the peerage in 1628 as Lord Reay. His grandson Aeneas commanded the Mackay regiment of the Dutch army and his family was ennobled by William V of Orange. Baron Eric Mackay van Ophemert became the twelfth Lord Reay and clan chief, his son, the thirteenth Lord Reay, becoming a naturalized British subject in 1938.

**Left: The Falls of Rogie
on the Blackwater are
in the territory of the
Mackenzies.**

MACKENZIE

Badge: An inflamed mountain with the Latin motto *Luceo non uro* (I shine, not burn).
Gaelic: *MacCoinnich.*

This clan is descended from Kenneth, son of Colin of the Aird, who was first Earl of Ross in the late thirteenth century. Murdoch, son of Kenneth, was granted Kintail in Wester Ross by David II in 1362. Intermarriage with Macdonalds linked the Mackenzies to the Lords of the Isles, but later they became deadly enemies and in 1491 the Mackenzies slaughtered the Macdonalds at Blair na Park. Support for the crown was rewarded by land, and by 1609, when Kenneth became Lord Mackenzie, the clan possessed all the territory from Ardnamurchan to Strathnaver. Colin, second Lord, became Earl of Seaforth in 1623. Forfeited for participation in the "Forty-Five," the chief was restored in 1788 after raising the Seaforth Highlanders.

MACKINNON

Badge: A boar's head with a deer's shankbone in its mouth, with the Latin motto *Audentes fortuna juvat* (Fortune helps the daring).
Gaelic: *MacFhionghuin.*

The clan claims descent from Fingon, great-grandson of Kenneth MacAlpin, but the earliest records show them in Mull as dependents of the Lord of the Isles, and the last abbot of Iona at the Reformation was John Mackinnon. The clan supported Montrose at Inverlochy (1645) and took part in the Jacobite rebellions for which the estates were forfeited. The chiefship passed in 1808 to a descendant of Donald Mackinnon who had emigrated to Antigua.

MACLACHLAN

Badge: A triple-towered castle with the Latin motto *Fortis et fides* (Brave and trusty).

Gaelic: *MacLachlainn.*

This clan was domiciled in Strathlachlan from early times, claiming descent from the ancient kings of Ireland. Documents from 1230 onward testify to successive chiefs, and in 1298 Gilleskel Maclachlan received a charter from John Baliol. The clan fought under Argyll and later Bonnie Dundee at Killiecrankie. The clan chief, serving as aide to Prince Charles, was killed at Culloden. The estates were forfeited but his son Robert obtained them again in 1749. Branches of the clan are also located in Lochaber, Perthshire, and Stirlingshire.

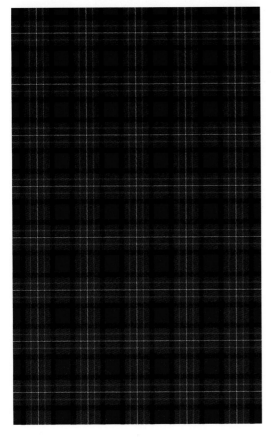

MACLAREN

Badge: The Virgin Mary and infant Jesus, with the Gaelic motto *Bi 'se Mac-an-t-slaurie* (Be thou the son of the crook).

Gaelic: *MacLabhruinn.*

Various accounts traced this clan back to Lorn, son of Erc, who came to Argyll in 503, or St. Lawrence, or three brothers who supported Kenneth MacAlpin from whom they obtained the lands of Balquhidder and Strathearn. The clan fought for the crown at Sauchieburn (1488), Flodden (1513), and Pinkie (1547); at other times they waged war on their neighbors. The clan was decimated at Culloden. The chief-ship was long in abeyance until John McLaurin, Lord Dreghorn (uncle of Burns's Clarinda) successfully petitioned for the title on grounds of descent from the Maclarens of Tiree.

Left: Looking toward
the Isle of Jura—
Maclean territory.

MACLEAN

Badge: A battlemented tower, with the motto "Virtue mine honor."
Gaelic: *MacGhille Eoin.*

Despite the Gaelic name meaning "son of the follower of St. John," the clan claims descent from *Gilleathain na Tuaidh* (Gillian of the Battleaxe) in the thirteenth century. From him were descended the brothers Lachlan Lubanach and Eachan Reaganach, respective founders of the Macleans of Duart and the MacLaines of Lochbuie in Mull. The clan fought at Harlaw (1411), Flodden (1513), Inverlochy (1645), Killiecrankie (1689), and Culloden where seven brothers gave their lives to protect the clan chief, to no avail.

MACLEOD OF HARRIS

Badge: A bull's head between two flags, with the Latin motto *Muros aheneus esto* (Be then a wall of brass).
Gaelic: *MacLeoid.*

Leod, son of Olaf the Black, derived his name from the Norse word *Ijot* (ugly). From his sons Tormod and Torquil came the two main branches of the clan, respectively the Macleods of Glenelg, Harris, and Dunvegan and the Macleods of Lewis, Waternish, and Assynt. Support for the crown gave *Siol Tormod* (the seed of Tormod) the lands of Glenelg (1343) and northwestern Skye (1498). The clan was almost wiped out at the battle of Worcester (1651), which explains why the clan was absent from the later Jacobite rebellions.

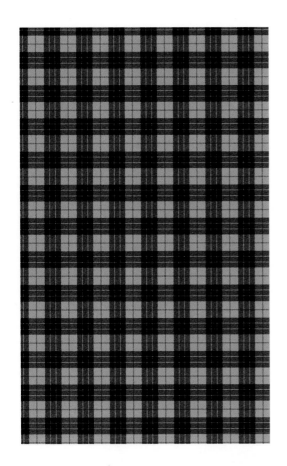

MACLEOD OF LEWIS

Badge: A radiate sun, with the Latin motto *Luceo non uro* (I shine, not burn).
Gaelic: *MacLeoid*.

This clan held lands in Lewis under the Lords of the Isles, but in the fourteenth century David II gave Torquil Macleod the barony of Assynt on the mainland, and over the years added estates in Gairloch, Raasay, and Waternish. The history of this clan is one of interminable feuds, not only with other clans but also with the Macleods of Harris.

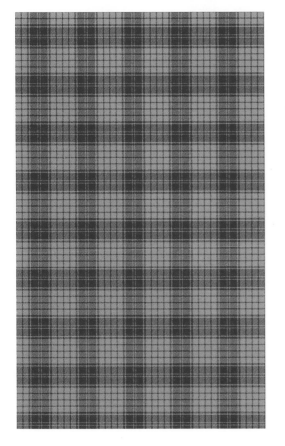

MACMILLAN

Badge: Hands brandishing a two-handed sword, with the Latin motto *Miseris succerere disco* (I learn to succor the unfortunate).
Gaelic: *MacGhilleMhaolain*.

The name translates as son of the servant of the tonsured one, indicating monastic origins. The clan was resident in the lands around Loch Arkaig by the twelfth century but then transplanted to Tayside. Later expelled, one branch moved to Knapdale and the other to Galloway, where they became staunch Covenanters. Daniel Macmillan, the Arran crofter who founded the great London publishing house, was the grandfather of Prime Minister Harold Macmillan (1957–63).

Left: The drawing room
of Dunvegan Castle on
Skye. The portrait is of
Sarah Macleod and her
son John Norman.

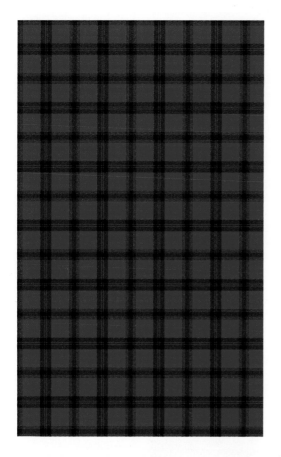

MACNAB

Badge: A savage's head, with the Latin motto *Timor omnis abesto* (Let fear be far from all).
Gaelic: *Mac an Aba.*

The name means "son of the abbot" and, like Macmillan, points to ecclesiastical origins, the clan claiming descent from the hereditary abbots of Glendochart. This once powerful clan backed the Macdougalls in their feud with the Bruce and suffered as a consequence, being deprived of most of their lands after Bannockburn. Their fortunes recovered in later centuries, supporting the Stewarts in the civil wars of the seventeenth century. Although the clan supported Prince Charles in 1745, the chief sided with the Hanoverians and kept his lands intact.

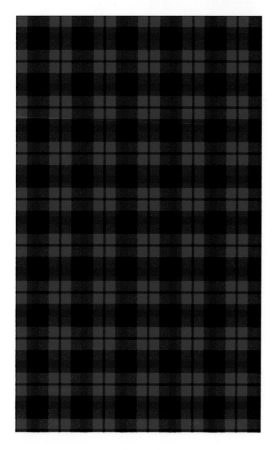

MACNAUGHTON

Badge: An embattled castle, with the motto "I hope in God."
Gaelic: *MacNeachdainn.*

The name means "son of the pure one," allegedly Nachtan Mor in the tenth century. This ancient Celtic clan was one of those transplanted from Moray after the uprising of the twelfth century, and resettled in Strathtay. From there they gradually expanded, acquiring lands on the shores of Loch Awe and Loch Fyne. The main line became extinct and the estates disposed of in 1691, and it was not until 1878 that the clan elected a new chief, Sir Alexander MacNaughtan of Bushmills, Ireland, a direct descendant of Shane Dubh who migrated in 1580.

MACNEILL

Badge: A rock, with the Latin motto *Vincere vel mori* (Conquer or die).
Gaelic: *MacNeill.*

Neil Og (young Nigel) received lands in Kintyre from Robert Bruce, and from this root came the two main branches of the clan associated with Barra and Gigha. They respectively allied themselves with the Macleans of Duart and the Lords of the Isles. As islanders, the Macneills were noted seafarers, a tradition maintained by the Macneill who designed the *Queen Mary* and the *Queen Elizabeth*. General Roderick MacNeill was forced to sell Barra in 1863, but in the mid-twentieth century the American architect Robert Lister Macneil purchased Kisimul Castle and restored it . His son, a professor of law at Cornell University, is the present chief.

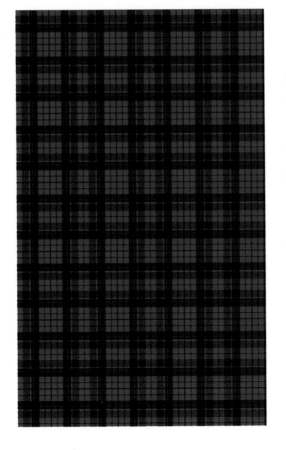

MACNICOL

Badge: A demi-lion rampant, with the Latin motto *Generositate* (With generosity).
Gaelic: *MacNeacail.*

The Macnicols or Nicolsons held lands in Coigach and Assynt granted by the Thane of Sutherland, but when Assynt passed by marriage of the Macnicol heiress to the Macleods, the Macnicols moved to Skye, settling at Scorrybreck. Thereafter the name of Nicolson features frequently in the history of that island as well as Lewis. The most famous clansman was John Nicholson (1822–57), veteran of many Indian campaigns.

MACPHERSON

Badge: A seated cat, with the motto "Touch not the cat bot (without) a glove."
Gaelic: *Mac a' Phearsoin.*

This powerful branch of Clan Chattan traces its descent from Murdoch, the Parson of Kingussie (hence the alternative Gaelic name of MacMhuirich), the family of Cluny emerging as the chief by the late sixteenth century. Involvement in the Jacobite rebellions resulted in forfeiture and exile, but the estates were restored to Duncan Macpherson in 1784 for services rendered in the American War.

MACQUARRIE

Badge: A mailed arm emerging from a crown and holding a dagger, with the Latin motto *Turris fortis mihi Deus* (God is a strong tower to me).
Gaelic: *MacGuaidhre.*

The name means "son of the proud man" but is a Gaelic rendering of the Norman Godfrey. The clan claims descent from *Siol Alpin* (the seed of Alpin) through a brother of Fingon, and occupied the western part of Mull and the island of Ulva. Lachlan, sixteenth of Ulva, entertained Johnson and Boswell on their tour of the Hebrides but was forced to sell his estates in 1778. Last chief of the Macquarries, he lived to the age of 103. Most famous clansman is Sir Lachlan Macquarrie, Governor of New South Wales and founder of Sydney.

MACQUEEN

Badge: A wolf rampant holding an arrow, with the motto "Constant and faithful."
Gaelic: *MacShuibhne*.

The name means "son of the good going," but points to a Norse origin and a progenitor named Sweyn. The castle and loch called Sween in Argyll are reminders of the ancient clan lands although Macqueens were also to be found in Skye, Lewis, and even St. Kilda.. The chief branch moved to Strathdearn in Moray and allied themselves to the Mackintoshes. Famous clansmen include Robert MacQueen, the infamous judge Lord Braxfield, and Finlay MacQueen, last of the St. Kilda cragsmen.

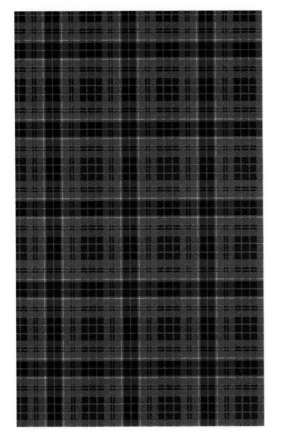

MACRAE

Badge: A hand grasping a sword, with the Latin motto *Fortitudine* (With fortitude).
Gaelic: *MacRath* (Son of grace).

The name has been traced back to a family living in the Beauly area in the twelfth century, transplanted to Kintail in Wester Ross in the fourteenth century where Fionnla Dubh had his seat at Eilean Donan. Although the Macraes were heavily involved in the civil wars of the seventeenth century, and fought heroically at Sheriffmuir (1715), they were not involved in later Jacobite rebellions. Ironically, their stronghold was destroyed after it was occupied by Spanish troops in the rebellion of 1719, but was restored in the twentieth century.

Left: Eilean Doran
Castle on the shore of
Loch Duich is in the
territory of the
Macraes.

MALCOLM

Badge: A silver tower, with the Latin motto *In ardua petit* (He aims at difficult things).
Gaelic: *Mac Mhaol Chaluim.*

The name means "son of the devotee of St. Columba" and shows the close connections with the MacCallums, but the name Malcolm was adopted in 1779 when Dugald MacCallum succeeded to the estate of Poltalloch. John Malcolm of Poltalloch was created Lord Malcolm in 1896. A branch of the Malcolms has been domiciled in Stirlingshire since the fourteenth century.

MATHESON

Badge: A forearm wielding a sword, with the Latin motto *Fac et spera* (Do and hope).
Gaelic: *MacMhathain.*

Known as the clan of the Bear, this ancient Celtic family held lands in Wester Ross and Sutherland. The story goes that they aided Kenneth MacAlpin in gaining the Pictish throne in 843. In more recent times the two main branches were the Mathesons of Lochalsh and Shiness, from whom respectively descended Sir Alexander and Sir James, both baronets who made vast fortunes in India and spent their money on estates in Ross-shire and Lewis. The latter was co-founder of Jardine Matheson of Hong Kong, now a global conglomerate.

MENZIES

Badge: A full-face savage head, with the motto "Will God I shall."
Gaelic: *Meinnearach.*

The progenitor of this clan was a Norman mercenary named de Meyners whose descendant, Robert, became Lord High Chamberlain in 1249 and held lands in Perthshire. The letter "z" is actually the medieval letter *yogh*, pronounced like a "y" or "g," hence the proper pronunciation of this name as "Mingies." Menzies of Culdares introduced the larch and the monkey puzzle tree to Scotland in the 1730s. Most famous clansman was Sir Robert Menzies, Prime Minister of Australia.

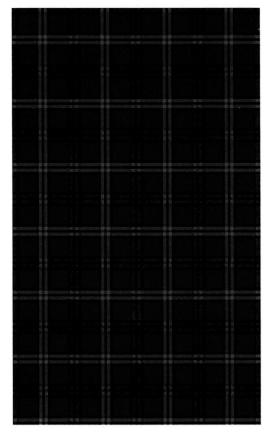

MONTGOMERY

Badge: A female figure holding a savage's head and an anchor, with the French motto *Gardez bien* (Look well).
Gaelic: *MacGumerait.*

Originally a Norman family from the Falaise district, the Montgomerys descend from Roger de Montgomery, regent of Normandy, who came with the Conqueror and was created Earl. His grandson, Robert, came to Scotland with Walter the Steward and received the lands of Eaglesham from David I. A peerage in the fifteenth century became the earldom of Eglinton in 1507, the family possessing considerable estates in Ayrshire and Renfrewshire. Most famous clansmen are Richard Montgomery, a general in the American War, and, of course, Field Marshal Viscount Montgomery of Alamein.

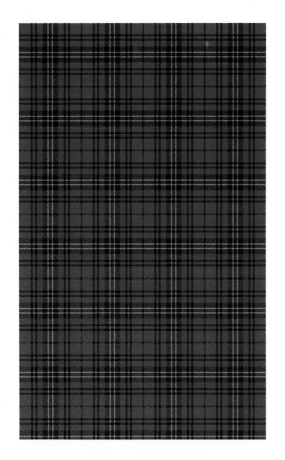

MORRISON

Badge: A coiled serpent, with the Latin motto *Praetia prudentia praestat* (In price, prudence predominates).
Gaelic: *MacGhille Mhoire*.

Despite the Gaelic name, rendered variously as "son of Maurice" or "son of the servant of the Virgin Mary," this clan is descended from Vikings shipwrecked on the shores of Lewis. The Morrisons of Habost were hereditary breves (lawyers) as late as the seventeenth century when they turned to the church. Although Morrisons are still plentiful in Lewis, branches of the clan settled in Harris, Uist, Skye, and Sutherland, but the Morrisons of Dunbartonshire, Perthshire, and Stirling are believed to have been a separate family. The most famous members of the clan were, perhaps, Marion Michael Morrison (1907–79) aka the "Duke"—John Wayne—and Jim (James Douglas) Morrison (1943–71) of the Doors.

MUNRO

Badge: A spread-eagle, with the motto "Dread God."
Gaelic: *Mac an Rothaich*.

The founder of this clan is said to have come from Roe in County Derry, but the earliest Munro on record is Hugh of Foulis who died in 1126. Robert Foulis supported Bruce at Bannockburn, and thereafter the clan was closely associated with the crown. In the seventeenth century the clan featured prominently in European wars, providing three generals and thirteen colonels for the armies of Gustavus Adolphus, as well as numerous officers of lesser rank. Most famous clansmen include Sir Thomas Munro, a noted Indian administrator, and James Monroe, fifth President of the United States. Also, a Munro is a Scottish peak over 3,000ft, from Sir Hugh Munro who classified them in 1891.

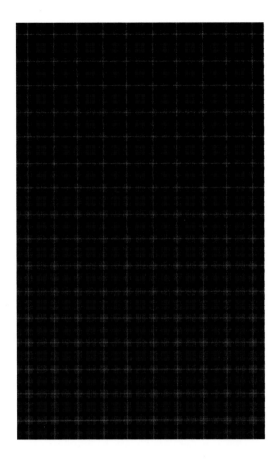

MURRAY

Badge: A demi-savage holding a dagger, with the motto "Furth fortune and fill the fetters."
Gaelic: *MacMhuirich*.

This powerful clan had its origins in the Celtic tribes of Moray but later acquired lands all over Scotland. Sir Andrew Moray was Wallace's chief lieutenant in the Battle of Stirling Bridge. Sir John of Tullibardine was created Lord Murray (1604) and Earl of Tullibardine (1606). His grandson claimed the earldom of Atholl (1629), later raised to a dukedom. Marriage with an heiress of the Stanley Earls of Derby brought the Isle of Man. John, third Duke, sold his title of Lord of Man to the crown in 1765. Other branches of the clan included the earls of Dunmore and Mansfield.

NAPIER

Badge: A right hand grasping an eagle's leg, with the Latin motto *Vincit veritas* (Truth prevails).

The name—which has no Gaelic equivalent derives from an ancestor who was in charge of the royal linen. John de Napier held lands in Dunbartonshire by the late thirteenth century and his descendants were prominent in the royal service, notably Sir Alexander of Merchiston who was Comptroller to James II, Lord Provost of Edinburgh, Vice-Admiral of Scotland and ambassador to England at various times. Most famous clansmen are John of Merchiston, inventor of logarithms and General Lord Napier of Magdala.

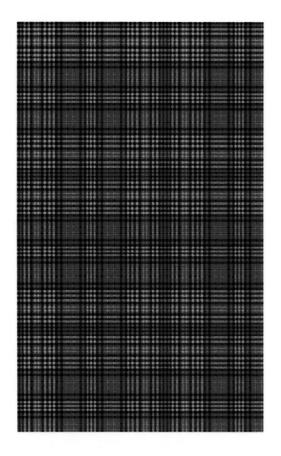

OGILVIE

Badge: A woman holding a portcullis, with the French motto *A fin* (To the end).
Gaelic: *MacGhille Bhuidhe.*

Gilbert, second son of Gilchrist, Earl of Angus, received the barony of Ogilvie from William the Lyon about 1163. His descendants became hereditary sheriffs of Angus and built the tower of Airlie. From a cadet of this family sprang the earls of Findlater and Seafield and lords of Banff. Sir James Ogilvie of Airlie was created Lord Airlie in 1491 and this was advanced to an earldom in 1639 but attainted in 1746 and not restored till 1826. Sir Angus Ogilvy, younger son of the ninth Earl, married HRH Princess Alexandra of Kent in 1963.

OLIPHANT

Badge: A gold crescent, with the motto "What was may be."

The name is derived from the elephant, symbolic of immense strength, and is derived from the Norman David de Olifard who came to Scotland in the retinue of David I in 1141. Sir Lawrence Oliphant was raised to the peerage in 1458. Later Oliphants of Gask were staunch supporters of the Jacobite cause. Carolina Oliphant (1766–1844), named after Prince Charles, is best remembered under her married name as Lady Nairne, the Scottish songwriter. This clan shares its tartan with the Melvilles, descended from another Norman in the entourage of David I who took his name from the manor of Mala Ville.

RAMSAY

Badge: A unicorn's head, with the Latin motto *Ora et labora* (Pray and work).

The Norman Simon de Ramsay was granted estates in Lothian by David I and founded the family of Dalhousie. Raised to the peerage in 1618, the Dalhousies advanced to an earldom in 1633. Successive generations had illustrious military careers. James, tenth Earl, was created Marquess of Dalhousie in 1849 and served as Governor General of India and Canada. He died in 1860 without issue and his titles passed to his cousin, second Lord Panmure. Famous clansmen include the poet Allan Ramsay and chemistry Nobel prize-winner Sir William Ramsay (1904).

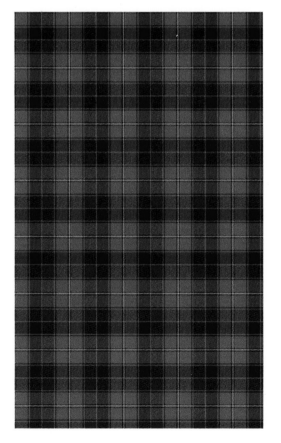

ROBERTSON

Badge: A hand holding an imperial crown, with the Latin motto *Virtutis gloria merces* (Glory is the reward of valor).
Gaelic: *MacDhonnachaidh.*

The Clan Donnachaidh claims descent from the Celtic earls of Atholl and derives its name from *Donnachadh Reamhar* (Stout Duncan) who led the clan to victory at Bannockburn, though the name Roberston comes from his descendant Robert Riach (grizzled) who apprehended the assassins of James I and was rewarded with the barony of Struan in 1451. The clan was an ardent supporter of the Stewarts throughout the civil wars and Jacobite uprisings. Sir William Robertson enlisted as a private soldier and rose to the rank of field marshal in World War I.

ROSE

Badge: A harp, with the motto "Constant and true."
Gaelic: *Rois*.

This clan of Norman origins takes its name from the flower and was settled in Strathnairn by the late twelfth century. Hugh Rose married the heiress of Kilravock which has been the clan seat ever since. Invariably supporting whichever government was in power, the Roses avoided the fate of so many others in the eighteenth century. The most famous clansman was Sir Hugh Rose, a veteran of many Indian campaigns, who rose to become a field marshal and was created Baron Strathnairn in 1866. J.A. Rose, a high official in the French Revolution, organized an escape route for emigres and was the original Scarlet Pimpernel.

ROSS

Badge: A right hand holding a laurel crown, with the Latin motto *Spem successus alit* (Success feeds hope).
Gaelic: *Ros*.

Modern thinking suggests that this clan, like Clan Rose, had a common Norman ancestry, although traditionally it is regarded as being one of the oldest Celtic families, taking its name from the ancient province of Ross. The progenitor of the clan is regarded as Fearchar *Mac-an-t-sagairt* (son of the priest), Laird of Applecross, who was created Earl of Ross in 1234. William, third Earl, led the clan at Bannockburn. The clan is also known as Clan Andrias, from MacGhille Aindreas, a chief predating the earldom which passed to the Lords of the Isles in 1424. The chiefship then passed to Hugh Ross or Rariches whose family acquired Balnagowan. Most famous clansmen are the polar explorers Sir John and James Clark Ross, and the pioneer of tropical medicine, Sir Ronald Ross.

SCOTT

Badge: A stag, with the Latin motto *Amo* (I love).
Gaelic: *Scotach.*

Uchtred *filius Scoti* (son of a Scot), who witnessed a charter of 1107, is regarded as the ancestor of this powerful Border clan whose main branches are the Scotts of Buccleuch and Balwearie. Sir Michael Scott of Balwearie, who died about 1300, was known as the "Wizard," actually the leading scientist of his time. From the senior line came the Earls and later Dukes of Buccleuch, a branch of which, the Scotts of Harden, produced Sir Walter, greatest of early nineteenth century novelists.

SHAW

Badge: A demi-lion holding a sword, with the Latin motto *Fide et Fortitudine*
(By faith and fortitude).
Gaelic: *Mac Ghille Sheathanaich.*

One of the leading branches of Clan Chattan, the Shaws claim descent from Shaw, great-grandson of Angus, sixth chief of Mackintosh, who received the lands of Rothiemurchus for services rendered at the clan battle of the North Inch (1396). The clan lost its lands and was dispersed in 1595. The Shaws of Tordarroch, known as Clan Aidh, were likewise a branch of Clan Chattan. The Lowland Shaws were prominent in Ayrshire and Renfrewshire, their most famous clansman being Sir James Shaw from Kilmarnock who became Lord Mayor of London.

**Left: Sea fog shrouds
the eroded stacks of
Duncansby Head in
Sinclair territory.**

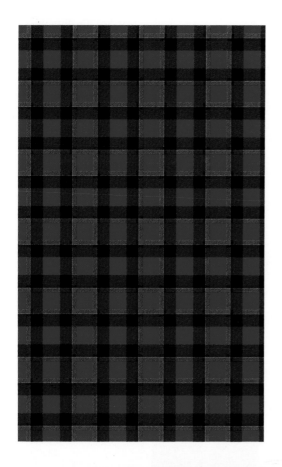

SINCLAIR

Badge: A cock, with the motto "Commit thy work to God."
Gaelic: *Mac na Ceardadh.*

This northern clan traces its origins to St. Clair in Normandy. William de St. Clair came with the Conqueror, while his grandson obtained the barony of Roslin from David I. Sir Henry supported Bruce and his son Sir William died with the Black Douglas in Spain. Henry Sinclair was created Earl of Orkney in 1379 while his grandson also became Earl of Caithness. Sir John Sinclair of Ulbster (1754–1835) was both an improving landowner and prolific poet, as well as a pioneer of demography and compiler of the first *Statistical Account of Scotland.*

SKENE

Badge: An arm issuing from a cloud and holding a laurel crown, with the Latin motto *Virtutis regia merces* (A palace is the reward of valor).
Gaelic: *MacSgian.*

According to William Skene, the Celtic historian, the clan was founded by a Struan Robertson who saved the king's life by slaying a wolf with his knife (*sgian*) and was rewarded with the lands of Skene in Aberdeenshire. John de Skene appears in the Ragman Roll (1296) and his grandson Robert, a supporter of Bruce, received a baronial charter from the king. When the direct line died out in 1827 the chiefship passed to James, fourth Earl of Fife, a nephew of the last chief. Most famous clansman was William F. Skene (1809–92), a prolific writer on Celtic Scotland who became Historiographer Royal for Scotland in 1881.

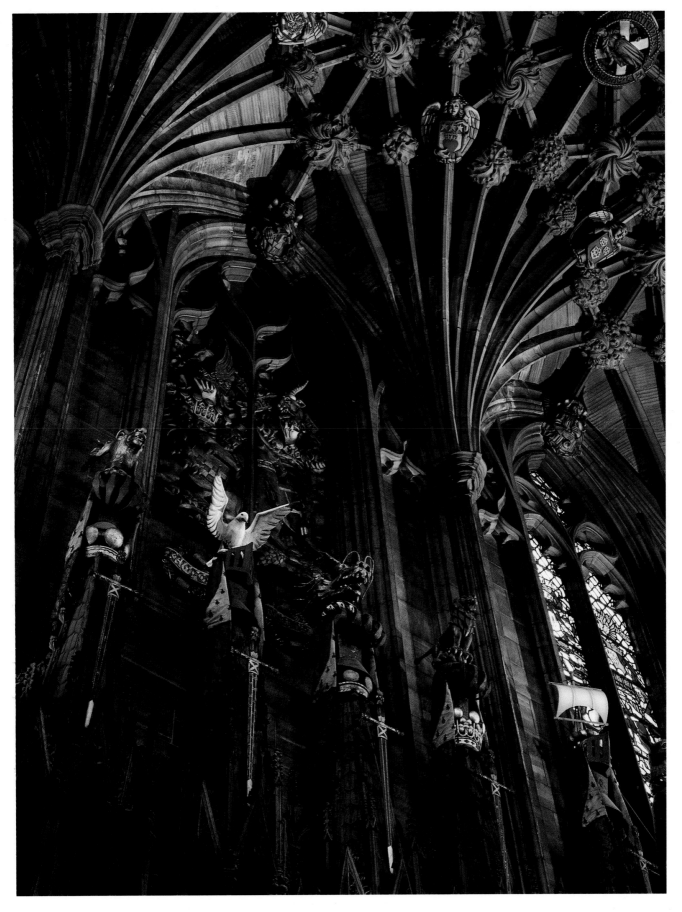

Left: Dunrobin Castle, seat of the Earl of Sutherland.

Previous page: The Thistle Chapel in St. Giles' Cathedral, Edinburgh.

STEWART

Badge: A seated lion holding a sword and sceptre, with the motto "In defens."
Gaelic: *Stiubhard.*

The royal clan is descended from Walter fitz Alan, appointed hereditary Steward by David I, with extensive lands in Renfrewshire. Walter, sixth Steward, married Marjorie Bruce, daughter of Robert I, and founded the dynasty which continues to this day. From the first three sons of Walter's uncle, Sir John Stewart of Bonkill, came the great earldoms of Angus, Lennox, and Galloway. The Stewarts also hold, or held, the dukedoms of Rothesay (now held by HRH Prince Charles), Albany, and Lennox, the marquessate of Bute, and the earldoms of Atholl, Buchan, Carrick, Menteith, and Strathearn as well as numerous lesser titles.

SUTHERLAND

Badge: A cat, with the French motto *Sans peur* (Without fear).
Gaelic: *Suthurlarach.*

The premier earldom of the British Isles was conferred in 1228 on William, Lord of Sutherland, great-grandson of Freskin de Moravia, ancestor of the Murrays. Support for the crown was reinforced by the marriage of the fourth Earl to a daughter of Robert Bruce. The earldom passed to the Gordons of Aboyne when the ninth Earl died without issue. From this warlike clan, perennially feuding with their Gunn and Mackay neighbors, was raised the Sutherland Highlanders, or 93rd Foot, in 1800, best remembered as the "Thin Red Line" at Balaclava in the Crimean War.

URQUHART

Badge: A demi-otter, with the Latin motto *Per mare per terras* (By sea and land).
Gaelic: *Urchurdan*.

Originally a branch of clan Forbes, the Urquharts take their name from the glen and castle near Loch Ness. Early in the fourteenth century William Urquhart became hereditary Sheriff of Cromarty and by marriage acquired lands in that district. Sir Thomas Urquhart, translator of Rabelais, fought on the Royalist side in the Civil War but died in 1660 on hearing the news of the Restoration. He also compiled a clan genealogy, showing himself as one hundred and forty-third in direct descent from Adam and Eve.

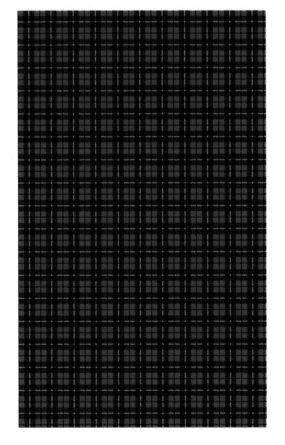

WALLACE

Badge: An armored right arm holding a sword, with the Latin motto *Pro libertate sperandum est* (For liberty we must hope).
Gaelic: *Uallas*.

To prove how ancient is this clan, early historians claimed descent from the Volcae of northern Gaul, but in fact the name merely described someone of Welsh (i.e. Strathclyde Briton) origin. The clan is descended from Richard Wallace who held lands in Ayrshire (Riccarton being derived from Richard's toun). His son Malcolm held the estate of Ellerslie near Kilmarnock, where his younger son William was born about 1270, not Elderslie near Paisley (a late eighteenth century invention). From the Wallaces of Ayrshire came the family of Craigie; Frances Wallace, later Mrs. Dunlop of Dunlop, was the "mother confessor" of Robert Burns. Other famous clansmen include General Lew Wallace, author of *Ben Hur*, the Pacific explorer Samuel Wallis, Poland's Solidarity leader Lech Walesa, and the late Duchess of Windsor (born Bessie Wallis Warfield).

THE SEPTS OF THE CLANS

There are numerous other variants of spelling.
Only the commonest versions are listed below.

Abbot(t), Macnab

Abbotson, Macnab

Abernethy, Fraser, Leslie

Adam(s), Gordon

Adamson, Gordon, Mackintosh

Addie, Addison, Gordon

Adie, Gordon

Ai(t)ken, Gordon

Airlie, Ogilvie

Airth, Graham

Alexander, Macalister, Macdonald

Allan, Grant, Macdonald, Macfarlane, Mackay

Allanson, Allison, Allyson, Macdonald, Macfarlane

Allardice, Graham

Alpin, Macalpine

Andrew, Ross

Angus, Macinnes

Arthur(son), Macarthur

Atkins(on), Gordon

Austin, Keith

Ayson, Mackintosh

Ayton, Home

Bain, Macbean, Mackay, Macnab

Ballantine, Campbell

Balloch, Macdonald

Balneaves, Murray

Bannatyne, Campbell, Stewart

Bannerman, Forbes

Barrie, Farquharson, Gordon

Bartholomew, Macfarlane

Bartlet(t), Macfarlane

Baxter, Macmillan

Bayne, Macbean, Mackay, Macnab

Bean, Macbean

Beathy, Macbean

Beaton, Macdonald, Maclean, Macleod of Harris

Begg, Drummond, Macdonald

Bell, Macmillan

Berkeley, Barclay

Berrie, Berry, Forbes

Bethune, Macdonald

Beton, Macdonald, Maclean, Macleod of Harris

Binnie, Macbean

Bisset(t), Fraser, Grant

Black, Lamont, Macgregor, Maclean

Blair, Graham

Bon(n)ar, Graham

Bontine, Bunten, Bunting, Graham

Bowie, Grant, Macdonald

Bowman, Farquharson

Buie, Grant

Boyce, Forbes

Boyd, Stewart

Boyes, Forbes

Brebner, Bremner, Farquharson

Brewer, Drummond, Macgregor

Brewster, Fraser

Brieve, Morrison

Brown, Lamont, Macmillan

Bryce, Macfarlane

Bryd(i)e, Brodie

Buchan, Cumming

Budge, Buie, Macdonald

Bulloch, Macdonald

Buncle, Home

Burdon, Lamont

Burk(e), Macdonald

Burnet(t), Campbell

Burns, Burnes, Burness, Campbell

Byers, Lindsay

Caddell, Campbell of Cawdor

Caird, Macgregor, Sinclair

Calder, Campbell of Cawdor

Calhoun, Colquhoun

Callum, Macleod of Raasay

Cambridge, Macdonald

Cargill, Drummond

Cariston, Skene

Carlyle, Bruce

Carmichael, Macdougall, Stewart

Carr(e), Kerr

Carrick, Kennedy

Carruthers, Bruce

Carson, Macpherson

Cassels, Cassilis, Kennedy

Cathal, Cathil, Macdonald

Cattanach, Macpherson

Cavers, Douglas

Caw, Macfarlane

Cessford, Kerr

Chalmers, Chambers, Cameron

Cheyne, Cumming, Sutherland

Christie, Christy, Christison, Farquharson

Clark, Clarkson, Clerk, Cameron, Mackintosh, Macpherson

Cle(a)ry, Cameron

Clement, Lamont

Clunes(s), Clunies, Mackenzie

Clunie, Cluny, Macpherson

Clyne, Sinclair

Coat(e)s, Farquharson

Cobb, Lindsay

Cochran(e), Macdonald

Collier, Colyear, Robertson

Colman, Buchanan

Colson, Macdonald

Combich, Stewart

Combie Mackintosh

Common(s), Cumming

Comrie, Macgregor

Comyn, Cumming

Connall, Conn(e), Macdonald

Con(n)ochie, Campbell

Connon, Gordon

Constable, Hay

Cook(e), Macdonald, Stewart

Cormack, Buchanan

Coulson, Macdonald

Cousland, Buchanan

Coutts, Farquharson

Cowan, Colquhoun
Cowie, Fraser
Craig, Gordon
Craigdallie, Macgregor
Craufurd, Crawford, Lindsay
Crerar, Macgregor, Mackintosh
Cririe, Macdonald
Cromar, Farquharson
Crombie, Gordon, Macdonald
Crookshanks, Cruikshanks, Stewart
Croom, Macdonald
Crosbie, Bruce
Crosier, Crozier, Armstrong
Crum, Macdonald
Cullen, Gordon
Currie, Macdonald, Macpherson
Dallas, Mackintosh
Daniel(ls), Macdonald
Darg(e), Gordon
Darroch, Macdonald
Davey, Davie, Davis, Davidson
Dawson, Davidson
Day, Dea, Davidson
Dean(e), Davidson
Deas, Deason, Davidson
Denoon, Campbell
Dennison, Dennistoun, Stewart
Deuchar, Lindsay
Dewar, Buchanan, Macnab, Menzies
Dey, Davidson
Dickerson, Dick(i)son, Keith
Dingwall, Munro, Ross
Dinsmore, Dunsmore, Murray
Dise, Skene
Dixon, Keith
Dochart, Macgregor
Dock, Drummond
Doig, Drummond
Doles, Mackintosh
Donachie, Campbell, Robertson
Donaldson, Macdonald
Donleavy, Buchanan

Donnell, Macdonald
Dorward, Gordon
Dougall, Macdougall
Dove, Dow, Buchanan
Dowie, Cameron
Dowall, Macdougall
Downey, Downie, Lindsay
Drain, Macdonald
Drysdale, Douglas
Duff, Gordon, Macduff
Duffie, Duffy, Macfie
Dullach, Stewart
Dunbar, Home
Duncanson, Duncan
Dunnachie, Robertson
Dunnel, Macdonald
Durward, Gordon
Dyce, Skene
Dye, Davidson
Eadie, Ed(d)ie, Edison, Gordon
Eaton, Home
Elder, Mackintosh
Easson, Esson, Mackintosh
Elder, Mackintosh
Enrick, Gunn
Esslemont, Gordon
Ewan, Ewen, Ewing, Macewen
Fair, Ross
Falconer, Keith
Farquhar, Farquharson
Federith, Sutherland
Fergus, Ferguson
Ferri(e)s, Farquharson, Ferguson
Ferson, Macpherson
Fife, Macduff
Findlay, Finlay, Finlayson, Farquharson
Findlater, Ogilvie
Fisher, Campbell
Fleming, Murray
Fordyce, Forbes
Forgie, Ferguson
For(r)est, Douglas, Macdonald

Above: Crinan Harbour,

Strathclyde.

Forrester, Macdonald

Forsyth, Lamont

Fotheringham, Lindsay

Foulis, Munro

France, Francis, Stewart

Fresell, Friseal, Frizell, Fraser

Frew, Fraser

Fullarton, Stewart

Fyf(f)e, Macduff

Galbraith, Macdonald, Macfarlane

Galdie, Gaillie, Gallie, Gunn

Ga(u)nson, Gunn

Gardiner, Gardner, Gordon

Garrick, Garrioch, Garriock, Gorodn

Garrow, Stewart

Ga(u)lt, Macdonald

Geddes, Gordon

Georgeson, Gunn

Gerrie, Gordon

Gibb, Buchanan

Gibbon, Buchanan, Cameron

Gibson, Buchanan

Gifford, Hay

Gilbert, Buchanan

Gilbertson, Buchanan, Cameron

Gilbride, Macdonald

Gilchrist, Maclachlan, Ogilvie

Gilfillan, Macnab

Gill, Macdonald

Gillanders, Ross

Gillespie, Macpherson

Gillies, Macpherson

Gilmore, Morrison

Gilroy, Grant, Macgillivray

Gilruth, Fraser

Glen, Glennie, Mackitosh

Glendinning, Douglas

Goodsir, Macgregor

Gorrie, Macdonald

Goudie, Macpherson

Gowans, Macdonald

Gowrie, Macdonald

Gracie, Farquharson

Grassick, Farquharson

Gray, Stewart, Sutherland

Greenlaw, Home

Gregor, Greg(or)son, Gregory, Greig, Macgregor

Greusach, Farquharson

Grewar, Drummond, Fraser

Grier, Grierson, Macgregor

Grozier, Armstrong

Gruar, Gruer, Drummond, Fraser

Gudger, Macgregor

Hadden, Graham

Haldane, Graham

Haliburton, Home

Hallyard, Skene

Hardie, Hardy, Farquharson, Mackintosh

Harper, Harperson, Buchanan

Harvey, Keith

Haw(e)s, Hawson, Campbell

Hawthorn, Macdonald

Haxton, Keith

Heggie, Mackintosh

Hendrie, Hendry, Henderson, Macnaughton

Heron, Macdonald

Hervey, Keith

Hewison, Hewson, Macdonald

Houston, Howison, Macdonald

Hughson, Macdonald

Huntly, Gordon

Hurrie, Hurry, Keith

Hutcheson, Hutchinson, Macdonald

Hutson, Hutton, Macdonald

Inch, Innes

Inches, Robertson

Inglis, Douglas

Ingram, Colquhoun

Innie, Innes

Inrig, Gunn

Isaac(s), Campbell

Isles, Macdonald

Iverson, Campbell

Jam(i)eson, Gunn, Stewart

Jeffrey, Macdonald

Jessiman, Gordon

Johnson, Gunn, Johnston, Macdonald

Jopp, Jupp, Gordon

K(e)ay, Davidson, Mackay

Kean, Keene, Gunn, Macdonald

Keddie, Kiddie, Ferguson

Keegan, Macdonald

Keighren, Macdonald

Kellar, Campbell

Kellas, Farquharson

Kellie, Kelly, Macdonald

Kendrick, Henderson, Macnaughton

Kenneth, Kennethson, Mackenzie

Kerracher, Farquharson

Key(s), Davidson, Mackay

Kilpatrick, Colquhoun

King, Macgregor

Kinnell, Macdonald

Kinnieson, Macfarlane

Kirkpatrick, Colquhoun, Douglas

Kirkwood, Macgregor

Kessack, Kissack, Campbell

Lachlan, Maclachlan

Laing, Colquhoun, Gordon, Macdonald

Lamb, Lambie, Lammie, Lamond, Lamondson, Landers, Lamont

Landale, Landels, Home

Lang, Gordon, Macdonald

Larnach, Stewart

Laurence, Lawrence, Maclaren

Laurie, Gordon

Law, Maclaren

Lawrie, Gordon

Lean, Maclean

Leaper, Leiper, Macfarlane

Leary, Cameron

Leavy, Buchanan

Leckie, Lecky, Macgregor

Lees, Macpherson

Leitch, Macdonald

Leng, Gordon

Lennie, Lenny, Buchanan

Lennox, Macfarlane, Stewart

Levack, Stewart

Lewis, Macleod of Lewis

Limont, Lamont

Lisle, Stewart

Lobban, Logan

Lockerbie, Lockerby, Douglas

Lombard, Stewart

Left: Glengarrisdale Bay on Jura: Maclachlan territory.

Lonie, Loney, Cameron

Lorne, Campbell

Loudoun, Campbell

Love, Mackinnon

Low, Maclaren

Lowden, Campbell

Lucas, Luckie, Lamont

Lumgair, Keith

Lumsden, Forbes

Lyall, Sinclair

Lyle, Stewart

Lyon, Farquharson

Macachounich, Colquhoun

Macadam, Macgregor

Macadie, Ferguson

Macaindra, Macfarlane

Macalaster, Macalester, Macalister

Macaldonich, Buchanan

Macaldowie, Cameron

Macalduie, Lamont

MacAllan, Grant, Macdonald, Macfarlane, Mackay

Macalonie, Cameron

Macandeoir, Buchanan, Macnab, Menzies

MacAndrew, Anderson, Mackintosh, Ross

MacAngus, Macinnes

Macara, Macgregor, Macrae

Macaree, Macgregor

Macartney, Farquharson

Macaskill, Macleod of Lewis

Maca(u)slan, Macausland, Buchanan

Macbeath, Macbeth, Macbean, Macdonald, Maclean

MacBeolain, Mackenzie

MacBrayne, Macdonald, Macnaughton

MacBride, Macdonald

Macbrieve, Morrison

MacCaa, Macfarlane, Mackay

MacCaig, Farquharson, Macleod of Harris

MacCainsh, MacCansh, Macinnes

MacCaishe, MacCash. Macdonald

MacCall, MacColl

MacCalman, MacCalmont, Buchanan

MacCambridge, Macdonald

MacCamie, Stewart

MacCammon, MacCammond, Buchanan

MacCardney, Farquharson, Mackintosh

MacCarron, Macdonald

MacCartair, Macarthur

MacCaskill, Macleod of Lewis

MacCasland, Buchanan

MacCaul, Macdonald

MacCause, Macfarlane

MacCaw, Stewart

MacCay, Mackay

MacCeallaich, Macdonald

MacClerich, MacChlery, Cameron, Mackintosh, Macpherson

MacChoiter, Macgregor

MacChruiter, MacChrutter, Buchanan

MacClair, Cameron

MacClintock, Colquhoun

MacCloy, Stewart

MacClure, Macleod of Harris

MacCluskie, Macdonald

MacClymont, Lamont

MacCodrum, Macdonald

MacColman, Buchanan

MacComas, Gunn

MacComb(e), Campbell, Mackintosh

MacCombich, Stewart

MacCombie, Mackintosh

MacConacher, Macdougall

MacConachie, Macgregor, Robertson

MacCondy, Macfarlane

MacConnach, Mackenzie

MacConnechy, Campbell, Robertson

MacConnell, Macdonald

MacConn(a)chie, Campbell, Macgregor, Robertson

MacCooish, Macdonald

MacCook, Macdonald

MacCorkill, MacCorkle, Gunn

MacCorkindale, MacCorquodale, Macleod of Lewis

MacCormack, Buchanan

MacCormick, Maclaine of Lochbuie

MacCorrie, MacCorry, Macquarrie

MacCoull, Macdougall

MacCowan, Colquhoun

MacCoy, Mackay

MacCracken, Maclean

MacCrae, MacCrea, Macrae

MacCrain, Macdonald

MacCraw, MacCreath, Macrae

MacCrie, Mackay, Macrae

MacCririe, Macdonald

MacCrimmon, Macleod of Harris

MacCrouther, Drummond

MacCrowther, Macgregor

MacCrum, Macdonald

MacCuag, Macdonald

MacCuaig, Farquharson, Macleod

MacCubbon, Buchanan

MacCuish, Macdonald

MacCulloch Macdonald, Macdougall, Munro, Ross

MacCunn, Macqueen

MacCutche(o)n, Macdonald

Macdaide, Macdaid, Davidson

MacDaniell, Macdonald

Macdavid, Davidson

Macdermid, Macdiarmid, Campbell

MacDonachie, Robertson

Macdonleavy, Buchanan

Macdowall, Macdougall

MacDrain, Macdonald

MacDuffie, Macfie

MacEachan, MacEachern, Macdonald

MacEaracher, MacErracher, Farquharson

MacElfrish, Macdonald

Maceur, Campbell

MacFadden, MaacFadyen, Macfadzean, Maclaine of Lochbuie

MacFall, Mackintosh

Macfarquhar, Farquharson

MacFater, MacFeat, Maclaren

MacFergus, Ferguson

MacGaw, Macfarlane

MacGeachie, Macdonald of Clanranald

MacGeoch, Macfarlane

MacGeorge, Buchanan

MacG(h)ee, Macghie, Mackay

MacGibbon, Buchanan, Campbell, Graham

MacGilbert, Buchanan

MacGilchrist, Maclachlan

MacGill, Macdonald

MacGilledow, MacGillegowie, Lamont

MacGillery, Cameron

MacGillevantic, Macdonnell of Keppoch

MacGillonie, Cameron

MacGilp, Macdonnell of Keppoch

MacGilroy, Grant, Macgillivray clan stone culloden

MacGilvernock, Graham

Macglashan, Mackintosh, Stewart

Macglasrich, Campbell, Macdonnell of Keppoch

MacGorrie, MacGorry, Macdonald, Macquarrie

MacGreusich, Buchanan, Macfarlane

Macgrime, Graham

MacGrory, Maclaren

Macgrowther, Macgregor

Macgruder, Macgruther, Drummond, Macgregor

Macgruer, Drummond, Fraser

MacGuaran, Macquarrie

Macgubbin, Campbell

Macgubbon, Buchanan

Macguffie, Douglas, Macfie

MacGuffog, Douglas

MacGugan, Macdougall, Macneill

MacGuaire, Macquarrie

Machaffie, Macfie

MacHardie, Farquharson, Mackintosh

MacHarold, Macleod of Harris

MacHay, Mackintosh

MacHendry, Henderson, Macnaughton

MacHowell, Macdougall

MacHugh, Macdonald

MacHutche(o)n, Macdonald

MacIan, Gunn, Macdonald

Macildowie, Cameron

Macilreach, MacIriach, Macdonald

Macilrevie, Macdonald

Macil(l)rick, Macilriach, Fraser

Mac(g)ilroy, Macgillivray, Grant

Macilvain, Macilwain, Macbean

Macilvora, Maclaine of Lochbuie

Macilvrae, Macgillivray

Macilvride, Macdonald

Macilwham, Lamont

Macilwraith, Macdonald

Macimmey, Fraser

Macinally, Buchanan

Macindeor, Buchanan, Macnab, Menzies

Macindoe, Buchanan

Macinory, Robertson

Macinstalker, Macfarlane

MacIsaac, Campbell, Macdonald of Clanranald

MacJames, Macfarlane

Mack, Home

MacKail, Cameron

MacKames, Gunn

MacKeachan, Macdonald of Clanranald

MacKeamish, Gunn

MacKean, Gunn, Macdonald

Mackechnie, Macdonald of Clanranald

Mackee, Mackay

Mackeggie, Mackintosh

MacKeith, Keith, Macpherson

MacKell, Cameron

MacKellachie, Macdonald

MacKellaig(h), Macdonald

MacKellar, Campbell

Mackelvie, Campbell

MacKelloch, Macdonald

MacKemmie, Fraser

Mackendrick, Henderson

Mackennal, Macdonald

MacKeochan, Macdonald of Clanranald

MacKerchar, Farquharson

MacKerlich, Campbell, Mackenzie

Mackerlie,Campbell

MacKerrachar, Farquharson

Mackerron, Grant

MacKerras, Ferguson

Mackersey, Ferguson

Mackessock, Campbell, Macdonald of Clanranald

Mackester, Hay

MacKiaran, Grant

MacKichan, Macdonald, Macdougall

Mackie, Mackay

Mackillican, Mackintosh

MacKillip, Macdonell of Glengarry

MacKim, Fraser

MacKimmie, Fraser

Mackinlay, Buchanan, Farquharson, Macfarlane, Stewart

Mackinnell, Macdonald

Mackinney, Mackinning, Mackinnon

Mackinven, Mackinnon

MacKirdy, Stewart

MacKissock, Campbell, Macdonald of Clanranald
Macknight, Macnaughton
Maclagan, Robertson
Maclaglan, Maclachlan
Maclairish, Macdonald
MacLamond, Lamont
MacLardy, Macdonald
Maclarty, Macdonald
Maclaverty, Macdonald
MacLaws, Campbell
MacI(e)ay, Buchanan, Stewart
MacLear, Cameron
Maclehose, Campbell
Macleish, Macpherson
Macleister, Fletcher
Maclellan, Macdonald
Maclennan, Logan
MacLergain, Maclean
Maclerie, Cameron, Mackintosh, Macpherson
MacLewis, Macleod of Lewis
MacLise, Macpherson
Maclintock, Colquhoun
Macliver, Campbell, Macgregor
MacLucas, Lamont, Macdougall
Macluckie, Macluke, Lamont
MacLulich, Macdougall, Munro, Ross
Maclure, Macleod of Harris
MacLymont, Lamont
Macmains, MacManus, Colquhoun
MacMartin, Cameron
Macmaster, Buchanan, Macinnes
MacMath, Matheson
MacMaurice, Buchanan
MacMenzies, Menzies
MacMichael, Stewart
MacMinn, Mackinnon
MacMonnies, Menzies
MacMorran Mackinnon
MacMunn, Stewart
MacMurchie. Buchanan, Macdonald, Mackenzie
MacMurdoch, Macdonald, Macpherson
MacMurray, Murray
MacMurrich, Macdonald, Macpherson
Macoultrie, Macmutrie, Stewart

Macnair, Macfarlane, Macnaughton
MacNee, Macgregor
MacNeilage, Macneill
MacNeish Macgregor
MacNelly, Macneill
MacNeur, Buchanan, Macfarlane
MacNider, Macfarlane
MacNie, Macgregor
MacNish Macgregor
MacNiter, Macfarlane
Macniven, Campbell, Cumming, Mackintosh, Macnaighton
Macnocaird, Campbell
MacNuyer Buchanan, Macfarlane, Macnaughton
MacOmie, Mackintosh
MacOmish, Gunn
MacOnie, Cameron
Macoran, Campbell
Macoshannaig, Macdonald
MacOstrich, Cameron
Macoul, Macowl, Macdougall
MacOurlie, Kennedy
MacOwan, Colquhoun
Macouat, Macowat, Forbes
MacOwen, Campbell
MacPatrick, Lamont, Maclaren
MacPeter, Macgregor
Macphail, Cameron, Mackintosh, Mackay
MacPhater, Maclaren
MacPhedran, Campbell, Macaulay
Macphee, Macphie, Macfie
MacPhilip, Macdonnell of Keppoch
MacPhun, Campbell, Matheson
Macquaker, Campbell
Macquattie, Buchanan, Forbes
Macquey, Mackay
Macquhirr, Macquarrie
MacQuistan, Macdonald
Macquoid, Mackay
Macra, Macrae
Macraild, Macleod of Harris
MacRaith, Macdonald, Macrae
MacRankin, Maclean
Macrath, Macrae
Macritchie, Mackintosh

Below: Glencoe is Macdonald territory. The Signal Rock in this "glen of weeping" traditionally marks the spot where the signal was given for the synchronized attack on the Macdonalds by the Campbells who had been enjoying their hospitality for the previous twelve days. The massacre was carried out by Campbell of Glenlyon on orders of William III, partly as an example to would-be rebels and partly because MacIan, the clan chief, had not sworn allegiance. On a point of honor, MacIan had delayed to the last moment but went to Fort William by mistake and was then ordered to take the oath at Inveraray, with a resulting and tragic delay. Only forty were actually killed in the raid, but their houses were destroyed and many others would perish from hunger and exposure.

MacRob(b), Gunn, Innes, Macfarlane, Robertson

MacRob(b)ie, MacRobert, Drummond, Robertson

MacRorie, MacRory, Macdonald

MacRuer, Macdonald

MacRurie, MacRury, Macdonald

MacShimmie, Fraser

MacSimon, Fraser

MacSorley, Cameron, Lamont, Macdonald

MacSporran, Macdonald

MacSuain, Macqueen

MacSwan, Macdonald, Macqueen

MacSymon, Fraser

MacTaggart, Ross

MacTause, Campbell

MacTavish, Campbell, Fraser

MacTear, Macintyre, Ross

MacThomas, Campbell

MacUlric, Kennedy

MacUlrig, Cameron

MacUre, Campbell, Maciver

Macvail, Cameron, Mackay, Mackintosh, Macpherson

MacVain, MacVane, Mackay

MacVanish, Mackenzie

MacVarish, Macdonald of Clanranald

MacVeagh, Macdonald, Maclean

MacVey, Macdonald, Maclean

MacVicar, Campbell, Macnaughton

MacVurie, Macdonald of Clanranald

MacVurrich, Macdonald, Macpherson

MacWalrick, Cameron, Kennedy

MacWalter, Macfarlane

MacWattie, Buchanan, Forbes

MacWhannell, Macdonald

MacWhire, Macquarrie

MacWhirter, Buchanan

MacWilliam, Gunn, Macfarlane

Macgrath, Macrae

Main, Gunn

Malcolmson, Maccallum, Macleod, Malcolm

Malloch, Maacgregor

Ma(g)nus, Gunn

Mann, Gunn

Manson, Gunn

Marchbanks, Marjoribanks, Johnston

Mark, Marquis, Macdonald

Marr, Gordon

Marshall, Keith

Martin, Cameron, Macdonald

Massey, Massie, Matheson

Masters, Masterson, Buchanan

Mathie, Matheson

Mavor, Gordon

May, Macdonald

Means, Menzies

Mechie, Me(i)kie, Forbes

Meikleham, MeiklemLamont

Mein(e), Menzies

Meldrum, Forbes

Melvin, Macbean

Mengues, Menzies

Mennie, Menzies

Menteith, Graham, Stewart

Meyners, Menzies

Michie, Forbes

Michison, Macdonnell of Keppoch

Middleton, Forbes, Innes

Miller, Macfarlane

Mill(s), Gordon

Miln(es), Gordon

Minn, Menzies

Minnus, Menzies

Mitchell, Innes

Moir, Gordon

Monach, Macfarlane

Monroe, Munro

Monteith, Graham, Stewart

Monzie, Menzies

Moodie, Moody, Stewart

Moray, Murray

More, Leslie

Morgan, Mackay

Morrice, Morris, Gordon, Buchanan, Morrison

Morton, Douglas

Mowat, Sutherland

Muir, Gordon

Munn, Stewart

Murchie, Buchanan, Macdonald, Mackenzie

Murchison, Buchana, Macdonald, Mackenzie

Murdoch, Murdoson, Macdonald, Macpherson

Mure, Gordon

Murphy, Macdonald

Mushet, Drummond

Mylne, Gordon

Neal, Neil, Neill, Macneill

N(e)ish, Macgregor

Neilson, Gunn, Mackay

Nelson, Gunn, Mackay

Nesbitt, Home

Nicol(l), Macnicol

Nisbet, Home

Niven, Cumming, Mackintosh, Macnaughton

Nixon, Armstrong

Noble, Mackintosh

Norman, Macleod of Harris

Nucator, Macgregor

Ochiltree, Campbell

Oliver, Fraser

O'May, Macdonald

Orr, Campbell, Macgregor

Parland, Parlane, Macfarlane

Paterson, Maclaren

Paton, Patton, Macdonald

Patrick, Lamont

Pattullo, Macgregor

Paul, Cameron, Mackintosh, Mackay

Paulson, Pawson, Mackay

Peden, Macdonald

Peter, Petrie, Macgregor

Philp, Philipson, Macdonell of Keppoch

Pinkerton, Campbell

Pitullich, Macdonald

Pole, Pol(e)son, Mackay

Pratt, Grant

Purcell, Macdonald

Pye, Pyott, Graham

Rae, Macrae

Rainy, Macdonnell of Keppoch

Randolph, Bruce

Rankin, Maclean

Rattray, Murray

Reid, Robertson

Reidfurd, Innes

Left: Loch Leven, in the territory of the Macdonalds of Glencoe. This branch of the clan was descended from *Iain Og* (young John), grandson of Angus Mor and half-brother of the first Lord of the Isles, who, in the fourteenth century, obtained lands in Glencoe on the shores of the Inverness-shire Loch Leven.

REFERENCE

Clan Societies

Most clans, and many septs have their own clubs and societies, usually worldwide but with various local chapters catering to clansmen in specific countries or regions. For details of these clan organizations contact:

The Council of Scottish Clan Associations, PO Box 27268, Houston, TX, 77227, USA.
The Scottish International Gathering Trust, 25 Dublin Street, Edinburgh, EH1 3PB (0131-557 4059).
The Scottish Tartans Society, Davidson House, Drummond Street, Comrie, Perthshire.
The Scots Ancestry Research Society, 3 Albany Street, Edinburgh, EH1 3PY (0131-556 4220).

Clan Museums

Clan Tartan Centre, Aviemore, Inverness-shire
Clan Donald Centre, Armadale Castle, Isle of Skye
Clan Donnachaidh Museum, Blair Atholl, Perthshire
Clan Gunn Museum, Latheron, Caithness
Clan Macpherson Museum, Newtonmore, Inverness-shire
Highland Tryst Museum, Crieff, Perthshire
Strathnaver Museum, Sutherland (Clan Mackay)

Further Reading

Adam, Frank: *The Clans, Septs and Regiments of the Scottish Highlands*; Edinburgh, 1970.
Bain, Robert: *The Clans and Tartans of Scotland*; Glasgow, 1953.
Bede, Tim: *Macroots: How to Trace your Scottish Ancestors*; Edinburgh, 1982.
Black, George F.: *The Surnames of Scotland: Their Origin, Meaning and History*; New York, 1946.
Brown, Keith: *Bloodfeud in Scotland 1573-1625*; Edinburgh, 1982.
Bruce, Duncan A.: *The Mark of the Scots*; Secaucus, NJ, 1996.
Campbell, John Lorne: *A Collection of Highland Rites and Customs*; London, 1975.
Cunningham, Audrey: *The Loyal Clans*; Cambridge, 1932.
Dallas, Ann: *The Badges of the Scottish Clans*; Edinburgh, 1954.
Donaldson, Gordon: *The Scots Overseas*; London, 1966.
Dorward, David: *Scottish Surnames*; Edinburgh, 1985.
Douglas, Ronald MacDonald: *The Scots Book*; Glasgow, 1935.
Drever, Helen: *Tales of the Scottish Clans*; London, 1989.
Dunbar, John Telfer: *The Official Tartan Map*; Edinburgh, 1976.
Ferguson, Joan: *Scottish Family Histories*; Edinburgh.
Fulton, Alexander: *The Scottish Clans and Their Tartans*; London, 1985.
Fulton, Alexander: *Scotland and her Tartans, the Romantic Heritage*; London, 1992.
Grant, Neil: *Scottish Clans & Tartans*; Edinburgh, 1987.
Grimble, Ian: *Scottish Clans & Tartans*; London, 1977.
Hamilton-Edwards, Gerald: *In Search of Scottish Ancestry*; Chichester, 1983.
Hanks, Patrick and Hodges, Flavia: *A Dictionary of Surnames*; Oxford, 1988.
Hunter, James: *Scottish Highlanders: A People and their Place*; Edinburgh, 1992.
Innes, Sir Thomas of Learney: *Scottish Heraldry*; Edinburgh, 1956.
James, Alwyn: *Scottish Roots*; Loanhead, 1981.

Jarvie, Gordon: *The Clans*; London, 1995.
Johnston, Tom: *Our Scottish Noble Families*; Glasgow, 1929.
Johnston, T.B.: *The Historical Geography of the Clans of Scotland*; Edinburgh 1899.
Kermack, W. R.: *The Scottish Highlands, a Short History*; Edinburgh, 1957.
MacDonald, Micheil: *Scots Kith & Kin*; London, 1989.
MacDonald, Micheil: *The Clans of Scotland*; London 1991.
Macgregor, Alexander A.: *The Feuds of the Clans*; Stirling, 1917.
Mclan, R.R.: *The Clans of the Scottish Highlands*; London, 1980.
Mackenzie, W.C.: *The Highlands and Isles of Scotland*; Edinburgh, 1950.
McLauchlan, Thomas: *History of the Scottish Highlands, Highland Clans and Highland Regiments*; Edinburgh, 1887.
MacLeay, Kenneth: *Highlanders of Scotland*; London, 1872.
Macleod, John: *Highlanders, a History of the Gaels*; London, 1996.
Martine, Roderick: *Scottish Clan and Family Names*; Edinburgh, 1992.
Matheson, Cyril: *A Catalogue of the Publications of Scottish Historical and Kindred Clubs and Societies*; Edinburgh, 1928.
Moncreiffe, Sir Iain of that Ilk: *The Highland Clans*; London, 1982 .
Moody, David: *Scottish Local History, an Introductory Guide*; London, 1986.
Moody, David: *Scottish Family History*; London 1988.
Pottinger, Don: *The Clan Headquarters Flags and Standards*; Edinburgh, 1977.
Roberts, John L.: *Feuds, Forays and Rebellions*; Edinburgh, 1999.
Scarlett, James: *The Tartans of the Scottish Clans*; Edinburgh, 1975.
Scottish Tartans Society: *The Guide to Scottish Tartans and History*; Edinburgh, 1977.
Semple, William: *The Scottish Tartans, the Badges and Arms of the Clans*; Edinburgh, 1945.
Sinclair, Cecil: *Tracing Your Scottish Ancestors*; Edinburgh, 1990.
Skene, William F.: *Celtic Scotland*; 3 volumes, Edinburgh, 1890.
Terry, Charles S.: *A Catalogue of the Publications of Scottish Historical and Kindred Clubs and Societies, 1780-1908*; Glasgow, 1909 .
Way, George: *Scottish Clan and Family Encyclopedia*; Glasgow, 1994.
Way, George: *Homelands of the Clans*; London, 1998.

Periodicals

The Highlander.
The Scottish Banner.
The Scottish Genealogist (quarterly, The Scottish Genealogical Society).